GENVENSIS. CHRISTOPHORVS COLVMBVS

IANVS

AFRICA

OPA

Albizola

Genoa

Cogoreto

THE DISCOVERER

S. F. McCarthy

Oconomowoc, Wis.

CHRISTOPHORVS·COLVMBVS·

CHRISTOPHER COLUMBUS

BORN AT GENOA, IN THE YEAR 1452,
DIED AT VALLADOLID, MAY 20, 1506.

*From an engraving by Fournier of the portrait (now in the Naval Museum
at Madrid), painted by Legrand from the Capriolo portrait.*

THE DISCOVERER

A NEW NARRATIVE OF THE LIFE
AND HAZARDOUS ADVENTURES OF
THE GENOESE
CHRISTOPHER COLUMBUS

BY ANDRÉ DE HEVESY

TRANSLATED FROM THE FRENCH BY
ROBERT M. COATES

THE MACAULAY COMPANY
NEW YORK · MCMXXVIII

PRINTED IN THE U. S. A.

CONTENTS

ILLUSTRATIONS

I. THE WEAVER'S SON

From the French border-line down to Genoa and beyond, the Italian coast lies bent and rocky, like a
rugged arm crooked about the sea. These are the borders
of the antique Ligurian, and the blue gulf, calm, serene
and wide, still focusses the land's attention as when the
Phoenician galleys roamed there, in the ancient days.

The bald, steep hills peer over one another's shoulders
out across the waters. The streams that seam their sides
rush foaming, as to a given destination, to the sea. The
little whitewashed towns that are sown along the hillsides,
among stubbly fields and clumpy greenery, turn all their
windows toward the gulf. Church steeples have a lighthouse look; the monastery bells call plaintively across the
waters. Even the houses seem to lean on their eminences,
as if only the stones that weight their flat, thatched roofs
kept them from sliding down into the sea.

Man, alone, turns stubbornly away, and bends his back

9

to master the ungrateful hills. The legions of the Cæsars, with whom his fathers battled, have gone: the Ligurian's struggle is now with the soil, and it is less successful. Farming fails him. He turns to the trades, and then to shop-keeping, until at last—like one of the pebbles in his swift streams—he is swept on downward, and turns, for very livelihood, to the sea.

.   .   .

The hamlet of Moconesi lies at the base of the Monte Ventorolo, among the rocky hills that rise eastward from Genoa. It was, in the fifteenth century, an appanage of the family of Fontanabona; it was also the home of a much humbler, peasant family, named Colombo. They were farmers, and had been for generations. But early in the century one of them had sickened of the soil. This one, Giovanni, came down to Quinto-al-Mare, a seaport town, as its name indicates, and a suburb of Genoa.

Little record remains of him, save that he was provident, and a father, for in 1429 we find him setting his son as an apprentice weaver, in the shop of Guglielmo di Brabante, at Genoa. The boy was named Domenico, and aged but eleven. He worked well, however, and learned industry and thrift (though later he forgot the lesson) at the looms of his Flemish master. He was twenty-two when he ended his apprenticeship. He celebrated the event by marrying

10

Suzanna Fontanarossa, daughter of a farmer in the nearby village of Bisagno.

Those were the days when a city's strength was in its walls. Genoa the Superb lay doubly fortified behind its hills and within a circle of fortifications whose battlements rose higher than its houses, hiding all but the church-spires, and the ships' masts in the harbor, and here and there the square towers crowning the mansions of Genoa's noble families—the Fregosi, the Giustiniani, the Fieschi, Pallavicini, Spinola, the Imperiali.

Watch towers, built half their height in cut stone and the rest in brick, guarded the city gates, and the sentinels there, in those turbulent times, were men chosen for their courage and vigilance. It was a mark of confidence when, in 1447, the Doge Giano Fregoso appointed Domenico to keep the watch-tower at the *Porto dell'Olivella*.

Such a post required attendance day and night. The sentinel's family lived with him in his tower, and it was there, in 1451, that the wife of Domenico Colombo began her preparations for child-birth. Motherhood was more a gamble then than it now is. Superstitions were many; there was even a popular game—the *redoglio*—in which bets were laid on the infant's sex. People said that if the mother were careful always to put on her right shoe first her child would be a boy, and perhaps Suzanna followed that rule: she gave birth, in one of the thick-walled rooms in the

Olivella Tower, to a son. She christened him in the name of him who had carried Jesus through the waters—the patron saint of travellers—Christopher.

The year was 1452—one year before the fall of Constantinople and the overthrow by the Turks of the Greek Empire.

The young Cristoforo Colombo—or, as the world has long since anglicized it, Christopher Columbus—was baptized in the little Church of San Stefano, administered by the Benedictine Monks. This was not his father's first dealings with the order, nor the last. The Weaver's Quarter of the city was under the Benedictine tutelage; in 1440, Domenico had rented from them a house and a meadow on the *Vicolo dell'Olivella*. And now, fifteen years later, the same order sold him a house and a plot of land on the *via del Mulcento*, hard by the Gate of San Andrea.

Two mighty crenelated towers, square-built of faced stone and joined by an ogival arch above a passageway framed by two marble pillars—that on the right crowned by a Grecian capital, the other by four eagles—the Porto di San Andrea stands today as it stood five hundred years ago. Beside this huge edifice, the home of Domenico crouched like a serf before his overlord.

A narrow door with blackened stone lintels opened directly from the street into the *bottega*—a long room, lighted by two windows, which served as work-shop, sales-

12

room and living quarters as well. A wooden staircase led up to the *caminata*—"the fire-place room"; here the meals were cooked, and the family sat warm through the long winter evenings. The elders slept in an adjoining chamber; the apprentices and children, under the attic roof and in a closet behind the shop.

In this house, Suzanna gave birth to four more children: Bartolomeo, Giovanni-Pellegrino, Giacomo and, last, a daughter—Bianchinetta.

Domenico had left his sentinel's post and returned to the craft of weaver. It made, however, little difference in the life of his son, Christopher. Born in the tower of the *Olivella*, he grew up in the shadow of the Gate of San Andrea. One can picture the boy at play beneath the mighty walls, or climbing to the platform at the tower-top, to stare down at the long ships drifting into port, with their sails furled and oars at rest for the mooring. And while he looked, the weather-beaten watchmen told him of other towns and other towers, and the far lands these ships had come from—Kaffa, Tana, Trebizond—each marking a step in the mighty strides the power of Genoa was making toward the lands of gold and spice and wonder in the East. The boy's mind had much to marvel at.

Already these hardy seamen of the Republic had made a highway through the dangers that lay beyond the Indies into China. So early as the thirteenth century, Pietro di

Lucalongo had built at his own expense a cathedral in Pekin. The red flag of Genoa flew in the mouth of the Euphrates where the ships rode at anchor, waiting for the overland caravans. Genoese trading posts were scattered all through Asia. Colonies about the Black Sea were held by force of arms against the furious attack of the infidel, so that the Banca di San Giorgio, the bank that governed the plutocratic Republic, ruled half the East besides, embarking navies and financing armies to defend its empire.

We can only imagine what echoes of these fantastic tales persisted in the child's brain—or what stirrings at his heart as he stood in the tower and watched the great sails rise and heard the sailors cheering as the fleet took way for the Orient—or what dreams and ambitions filled him when he ran homeward down the narrow streets, and a gust of wind would come blowing in from the harbor, setting the washlines flapping like banners, and filling the sordid neighborhood with the salty breath of the sea.

. . . .

The weavers' guild maintained a tutor to instruct their children. Christopher, perhaps, had some schooling from the Benedictine monks as well; in later life, at any rate, he showed himself able to write Latin with passable fluency. But in that day, workmen's children were set early to the

14

father's trade. Before he was twelve, Christopher had entered his apprenticeship.

Domenico tended his looms at home. The boy ran errands, carded the wool, fetched materials to the shop, and delivered the finished fabric to the ships taking on cargo in the harbor. Soon both he and his brother Bartholomew were earning their living as *carminatores*: that is, journeyman weavers.

They formed the usual friendships of their class in life; Christopher, all his life through, was to have a gift for making friends. The will and testament of one Nicolo Monleone, made at this period, bears his signature as a witness before the notary. The other signers were a shoemaker, a napper, and three tailors. His cousins: Gianetto, Matteo, Tomaso and Amighetto were all weavers or wool-merchants.

Meanwhile, a change had come over the father, Domenico. He, who had been twice a weaver, and a tower guardsman, now felt himself outgrowing his profession. Perhaps something of the restlessness that was forever to animate his son had its beginning in his own blood; if so, it was less well-directed. He bought wine, and sold it again; he dealt in cheese and dabbled in real estate, hurrying, like a rustic promotor, to Quinto-al-Mare and back to Savone, and then to Genoa.

At last, in 1470, his enterprise found outlet in a wine-shop. The little front room of the house on the *via del Mulcento* was cleaned out and refurbished. Wool, cheese and looms were stored away and wine-casks took their place. Domenico Colombo was now set up as inn-keeper.

Many of these one-room wineshops still remain in Italy; their aspect has not changed. A rough table, chairs, and the barrels form the furnishings, and the men sit, proprietor and customers together, each with a mugful of rank black wine at his elbow. It is a common meeting-ground for all the trades. Shop-keepers, weavers, tailors, and sailors swap tales of market-town and port, while the glasses brim, and are emptied. And with the wine, the men's minds are lit by an imagination that clouds and flares by turns, like the old-fashioned oil lamp that illuminates the room, and the tales they tell develop queer patterns where their own adventures mingle confusedly with the great deeds of ancient heros, wandering into far-off lands.

Young, yellow-haired Christopher and the sturdy brother Bartholomew filled the wine-pitchers and served the tables, and listened with the shy interest of boys. It was thus, perhaps, in their father's tavern that they first heard the magic name: *Cypango*—Land of Gold.

But if the evenings were given over to mythical adventurings toward fabulous golden hoards, there were realer needs, by day, to be satisfied. Domenico was growing older, depending more and more on his sons. Soon, Christopher, the eldest, became a formal partner in the business; in 1470 he ordered wine from one Pietro Bellesio, vintner at Porto-Maurizio, and the payment—forty-eight lire— was contracted in his name. His first sea-faring began in such transactions, coasting down to the vineyards along the littoral, and beating back again with the light sloop loaded with the heavy barrels.

But the truth is, in these speculations Domenico was stretching his credit too far. He boasted that he was none of your pinch-penny traders. He gambled on the future, and let the present take care of itself. He married his daughter, Bianchinetta, to a neighboring cheesemonger, Giacomo Bavarello, promising a dowry which was never paid until, at his death, the house on the *via del Mulcento* was sold to satisfy the obligation. Meanwhile, his accounts had fallen into inextricable confusion. Creditors clamored for payment, and the laws of Genoa, that republic of business men, had a hard bite for the defaulter. In 1470, Domenico Columbus was imprisoned for debt.

He was freed only upon solemn contract to repay the creditor—Girolamo del Porto—who had caused his arrest. Christopher, too, was made responsible for the father's debt.

In such conditions the young weaver lived and struggled until 1473. The life, and perhaps his father's character,

17

had a share in his decision, finally, to emigrate. There seems, certainly, to have been little love lost between the two. At any rate, in later years Christopher, though he gave proof of a deep love for his brothers, showed a marked indifference to the fate of his father, though the latter lived long, almost to the century's end.

The boy was twenty-two, when he left Genoa. Though later he returned to his native city on several occasions; though, still later, in Spain and struggling against poverty and depression, he made melancholy reference to his home, it would seem that his break with the miserable life of the *via del Mulcento* was more definite than a mere bodily leave-taking: it was a departure of the soul and spirit as well.

The truth is, we can say of him honestly what is so often said slightingly: he felt himself above his station. There is a mystery about such matters. Somehow, the buxom farmer-girl Suzanna, and the feverishly vacillating Domenico had begotten a creature of mind and will, courage and imagination—in a day when weavers' sons were supposed neither to have will, imagination, courage nor mind.

So it was perhaps not only pride, but expediency as well, that made him cast a veil over his low birth. Sometimes he ignored the question entirely; more often, he hinted vaguely at a connection with various noble families;

18

occasionally, in his letters, he referred to missions and posts of confidence—now obviously fabricated—entrusted to him by kings and princes. His son, Don Fernando, with the added sting of illegitimacy to spur him, continued the deception with less reason, but greater persistency. With unnecessary insistence and suspicious vagueness, he expatiates, in his *Historie*, on his father's high connections, denying rumors that he was a mechanic, and complaining bitterly when a curious *Psalterium Octuplex Augustini Justiniani*, published in Genoa, 1516, asserted that the Admiral was *"vilibus ortus parentibus"*—born of lowly parentage.

In those days, and especially in Spain, where chivalry was at its final apogee, Columbus had to bolster his merits with his blood. He could probably not otherwise have succeeded. But today we see him as more admirable, and find his achievement the more remarkable, knowing that it was as a young workingman, of poor education and humble family, that he began his amazing career.

In fact, viewed in that light, his success begins to verge on the incredible. Hardly half a century before, another peasant, Joan of Arc, had to perform miracles before she could gain the ear of a king. Columbus achieved it by his own will, aided by a series of fortunate events, the first of which was the circumstance of his birth, propitious in time and place. Since the shaping of his character and the formation of his ambition owed much in their development to his early life at Genoa, it might be well briefly to consider that life, and note its tendencies.

In those days, the sources of information were quite different from today. Books there were none, save the manuscripts or their rare printed copies, mostly of chronicles or religious commentaries, which only the nobleman, or the wealthiest commoner, could own. No one, among the common folk, could read, and if they could, their practical information would not have been much the greater.

History, or the study of contemporary events, had not yet been formalized; both lived in the spoken word—the call of the town crier, the tale of the traveller at the inn, the sermon of the priest in the pulpit.

So the roadway, then, filled the place of our newspaper —and news, by the road, was a weary time in coming. Monks, drovers and townsmen gathered at the cross-roads to interrogate the wayfarer. The nobleman in his castle listened eagerly to messengers, bringing report of cities that lay weeks, even months behind him.

Of such stuff were fashioned their ideas of history and geography—a mixture of fantasy and legend, crusted over the kernel of truth at the core. Still more vague, was the road that led into the past. The men who had travelled there fell into dust and vanished; tales of them and their doings continued like ghosts on the way.

20

Marco Polo, the Venetian, who had wandered throughout all Asia two centuries earlier, remained the most vivid of these phantom heroes. His tales of strange animals, fantastic peoples, mighty kings and glittering courts, bizarre enough in themselves, grew still more fabulous, with the telling and retelling, in the popular mind. His adventures had turned all men's eyes to the East. Children of Columbus' time were fed with him, as they are today with Robinson Crusoe. Only, his tales had a basis in the authentic. Young men could dream of following in his footsteps. Older men could—and did—attempt the journey.

So the whole movement of the mind was toward far lands and distant places, and nowhere was the impulse stronger than in Genoa, that port where legend blended with accomplished fact, and each ship brought cargoes that might have come from the rainbow's end, while their crews came ashore full of strange tales and exotic souvenirs. The Florentines had a song about their merchants' homecoming, but it might well have been for the Genoese to sing its lines:

> Dagli estremi confin di Gallicutta
> Con diligenza e cure
> Abbiam piu spezierie di qua condutte . . . .

"From far Calcutta's border faring,
  Though care and trouble haunt the way,

Our scented cargo boldly bearing
We come with spices from Cathay . . . ."

And while the Christian trader roamed through Asia, the same impulse drew the Oriental merchant on to Genoa, in search of barter.

The streets were lined with arcaded booths where the guilds and trading corporations of every nation met and conducted their affairs. Here blond dealers from the Hanseatic towns haggled with the dark Catalonians. Frenchmen, Portuguese and Flemish rubbed shoulders with Armenians, captains from Barbary, and Turkish traders from the Levant. The workaday world took on something of the color of fairyland, as the native gutteral of the Ligurian dialect was threaded through with Spanish terms and Arabic locutions, and in the market place where housewives bought their butter one would see a train of slaves—pale Circassian women, slender dancing girls of Tartary—brought from the trading posts of Tana at the mouth of the River Don, to the Genoese auction block. They went from there into the homes of the nobles, where slaves were badges of patrician luxury, like white mules, or a silver table service.

Small wonder that such magnificence brought heady dreams to the young wool-weaver. His childhood had been spent at the very cross-roads and focus of the Eastern trade. It was but natural that his ambitions should reach out in that direction.

All about him breathed of the East. Italy, center of civilization, focus of wealth, lighthouse of ideas for the Occident, had all its art and manufacture tinctured by the influence of the Orient. Workers in Egyptian marble and Syrian ceramics transferred their studios to the Peninsula, seeking the patronage of a people who as early as the thirteenth century had known the exotic pattern of fabrics and tapestries brought from Asia.

The fall of Constantinople, warehouse and trading center since the eighth century for India and China, had given all its former power to the Italian towns, augmenting their population and their resources as well when thousands of Byzantine traders sought refuge there from the Turkish influence, until now Venice, Florence, Lucca and Genoa supplied the whole Christian world with spices, silks, pearls and precious stones from the East.

The wealthy and cultured people of these thriving cities of Italy were, then as now, passionate collectors and antiquaries. Jewelry, enamels, porcelains, books, manuscripts, wrought copper from Damascus—all these were ardently sought and treasured. From the corner grocer with his stock of spices to the nobleman at the head of the trading company, the minds of all fell on the magic East.

And though year by year its products became more

THE CITY OF GENOA.

FROM A SIXTEENTH CENTURY WOOD-CUT.

"Genoa the Superb lay doubly fortified behind its hills and within a circle of fortifications whose battlements rose higher than its houses, hiding all but the church-spires, and the ships' masts in the harbor, and here and there the square towers crowning the mansions of Genoa's noble families. . . ."

24

costly and trade more difficult, the current of thought that had set in its direction strengthened rather than diminished. Fifteenth Century Italy was too powerful a nation to be lightly halted by no matter what obstacle. The more difficult of satisfaction, the wider the contagion of aspiration spread. Like the sap in the tree, it fed all branches of life and industry. Leonardo da Vinci, Florentine sophisticate, and the untaught youngster of the *via del Mulcento* at Genoa throbbed alike with at least one ardor—a consuming curiosity toward the unknown East.

. . .

In those days, the custom was to give a young man going a journey his *denario a Dio*—God's farthing—as an omen of good fortune on the way. That the improvident Domenico could spare even that, in the hard time that had come upon him, is improbable, but Italy herself had given to Christopher a golden gift—the explorer's impulse, the urge toward the Unknown. He was to invest it well.

II. HE LIFTS HIS EYES

Sailors, even more than poets, write their histories in water; their mark is impermanent as the trace of a ship's passing. Later, the name of Columbus was to echo even across oceans. But at the age of twenty-two, Christopher was no more noteworthy than hundreds of other young Genoese who turned to the sea for livelihood, and no more note remains of his life in this period than of the other hundreds.

He himself tried, but not always quite honestly, to meet this deficiency. His record of this part of his life was intended rather to impress his contemporaries than to aid the historian, and when once the palpable discrepancies in his and Fernando's fictions are revealed, the details of his first few years of sea-faring remain as much a mystery as before.

Thus, much later, he wrote King Ferdinand of Aragon: "The good King Reinel (René), who is no longer living, sent me to Tunis, to capture the galley 'La Fernandina', then taking on supplies in the harbor"—implying that thus early in life he had embarked on the bold career of a privateersman.

It may seem that a piratical past was not a very high one to invent for himself, while he was about it. But in those days piracy was a quite legitimate, even an honorable profession. The gentlemen who followed it did so by the authority of letters-patent from their princes. They were the soldiers of fortune, the voluntaries of the sea, warring only with the enemy—in which they differed from the free-booters, who ravaged friend and foe alike.

The veteran privateersman was one who could blend hot fury with cool resourcefulness. He must plan his attack with slow care, but execute it with dramatic suddenness. He must leap like a lion as the vessels grappled, yet keep an icy calm for the deck-combat that followed. Finally, when the prize was won, and the dead had been flung over the taffrail and the living gathered to divide the spoils, he must be a commander able to outface his reckless crew and tame their wildness. It is not very likely that young Christopher, so early in his experience, knew such adventures other than at second hand, as the older sailors spun their yarns. It becomes still less likely if we remember that he was but nine years old when, in 1461, King René embarked on his last naval campaign!

His anecdote is interesting for another reason, however. "On arriving at the island of San Pedro, in Sardinia," he goes on, "I learned that there were two ships and a caracca with the galley, which so alarmed the crew that they resolved to proceed no farther, but to return to Marseilles for another vessel and more people. Upon which, being unable to force their inclination, I yielded to their wish, and *having first changed the points of the compass*, spread all sail, for it was evening, and at daybreak we were within the cape of Carthagena, while all believed for a certainty that they were going to Marseilles." On the first trip to America, he deceived his crew in a similar fashion, to the same end.

As a matter of fact, however, Christopher began his career in much more peaceful surroundings. In Genoa the State did not, as among the Venetians, control its merchant marine. Sea-trading was an individual affair, and the Republic entered only in that it supervised the ships' armament and named—through its *Officium Gazarie*: a sort of Naval Ministry—the admiral in command of each fleet of traders.

The exact date of his voyage is indefinite. In the year 1474, a fleet commanded by Gioffredo and Nicolo Spinola sailed for the Levant. Columbus went either with them or, in the year following, with the fleet of Paolo di Negro and Baldassare Squarciafico. Di Negro held the monopoly for importing wheat to Genoa; on this occasion he had been charged by the government to bring provisions and reinforcements to an outpost on the island of Chios, menaced by the Turks.

Columbus' name does not appear among the sailors on the roll of either of these fleets. He embarked probably as a clerk, serving one of the ship-owners. Such a position carried with it opportunities that, ashore, would have been denied the son of a simple inn-keeper. The sea is always a great leveller of persons. Even in that day, the arrogance of the mighty Genoese noble toward his humbler fellows could not entirely withstand the intimacy of a long voyage. His hauteur softened into comradeship.

And so Christopher, entering the service of the great, gained a broader understanding and a higher standard of thought. He listened to these captains of trade and of adventure as they talked of politics in the Mediterranean and wars in Asia, and how the eastern trade was hindered thereby; of the need for gold, and the crisis in foreign exchange; of the search for new routes to the Orient, where undiscovered countries, rich in gold, were hinted.

Buying wool and selling cloth remained his means of livelihood, but now his thoughts and aspirations had risen toward higher levels. His comrades' lives revolved between salt beef and hardtack aboard ship, and feasting and debauchery ashore, but the young Genoese watched

29

with clear eyes and remained apart, dreaming of greater wealth, more beautiful women, more honorable achievement.

The tales he had heard in childhood, on the watch-tower, were weighed in his mind with the information and experience his voyages were giving him. His horizon widened to the sea's width, and he stared out at it, through the silent nights, striving to pierce its unknown borders. Somewhere, in that great immensity, he would seek and find his fortune.

The immensity of that ocean, and its tragic awe, can hardly be conceivable to us now. Broad as it was, it seemed the broader for the mystery that clouded it. Black as it was, it seemed the blacker for the horrors with which men's superstitious minds had peopled it. And as yet, in the night of ignorance that reigned there, the light of all man's knowledge died like a torch, almost at its borders.

Sailing ships, hardly larger than a Banks fisherman to-day, ranged through the Mediterranean, and up along the western coast of Europe. Clumsy galleys, each one a floating hell to the double row of prisoners chained to the oars between-decks, coasted across to Africa and around the shores of Spain. But beyond this little circle stretched the great dark waste which the mariners called the "Ocean-Sea", remote and unapproachable as the stars,

30

swimming with monsters, filled with terror, breathing of death.

The sea stretched flat, unending, to the borders of Infinity; the souls of the dead alone could come to its farther shore, where lay the Terrestrial Paradise. So some argued, but there were others who held that it curved, like the slope at the lip of a precipice; once started, the descent was steeper and steeper, and no man could remount its side again. Thus it was that many brave explorers had vanished from men's knowledge, as had the Genoese sailors Tedisio Doria and Ugolino Vivaldi, of whom old tales still were told, in the night watches.

So the world was pictured in the eyes of the common people; to the learned mind it was but little less dreadful. Even Pietro Quirino, the scholarly Venetian, could say nothing of what lay beyond the Pillars of Hercules, save that these were "places uncharted, horror-filled".

The students, and the patrician amateurs of the day, had, certainly, a smattering of the ancient knowledge of the Arabic astronomers. They had access, too, to the speculations of antiquity and the accounts of the earlier explorers. Ship-owners and ship-captains had their maps and chart books, engraved with an art only rivalled by their inaccuracy, on which the known and the unknown mingled in picturesque confusion. But no man had yet dared to put them to the test.

31

THE DISCOVERER

Il ne fault plus s'amuser aux pratiques
De ces revueurs cosmographes antiques
Qui n'ont cogneu la moitié de ce monde. . . .

> "The maps the ancients drew
> Ridiculous may seem;
> Remember, half they knew
> Was more than half a dream. . . ."

So, a century later, wrote Jacques Hamelin Lochois. He might have added that the dreams were troubling ones; all the world was avid for knowledge of the unknown.

Poor folk talked of it in the taverns; the learned speculated on it in their studies. Kings made cosmography their hobby. Princes and prelates pored over maps and gravely published their deductions. Charting the universe became an exercise in didactic, bearing the same relation to fact as alchemy to physics, and the aristocrat followed it with a similar enthusiasm. Justius of Ghent, painting King Ptolemy, shows him a student of the art. Garbed in a flowing blue robe, trimmed with jewels, he holds a globe of the world aloft as one might hold a torch, and the eyes look out under a heavy brow, as if piercing a veil of mystery. How, then, did the weaver's son dare lift his eyes to such a knightly occupation?

His equipment, certainly, was slight. Asia was his aim, but his picture of it, and the one he retained to the end of his days, was one of naïve fantasy. Colored by his childhood tales of Marco Polo, themselves distorted by two centuries of telling, the East he visioned was a land more miraculous than real. Larded with rubies, glittering with diamonds, smelling of spices and aromatic oils, the Orient to him became a kind of fairyland of man's desire.

There the elephant roamed, and the fabled unicorn. There palaces, bursting with treasure, lay hid in forests fragrant with strange, sweet-scented woods. Tartary was there, and beyond it lay the realm of the Grand Khan, Prince of Princes, his throne in the City of Cathay. Still farther, beyond the farthest shore of this monstrous continent, lay Cypango—the Island of Gold.

This was his picture of the unknown world; of the known, he knew but little more. His trade had taught him a little of the aspect of Europe. The talk in his father's inn had told him of the factions among nations, their cities and their people. Coins of all countries, then, passed current everywhere. He had handled them, noting the profiles of the foreign kings. Not even now did he dream that one day he would stand before them, weighing their words with a courtier's anxiety, while his fate waited on their decision.

For the rest, he listened to the talk of the sailors, learning what he might from the conversations of the merchants and the captains. Meanwhile he lost no opportunity to complete his training as a seaman. Soon he could read a nautical chart, and had grasped the elements of astronomy. So far, no expedition of his had passed beyond the waters of the Mediterranean, but already his mind was straying toward the distant reaches beyond. It was perhaps as well for his determination, that the mind was young, the hardier for his ignorance and his solid peasant blood. It gave him the greater courage to face the unknown.

For the moment, his mind seethes in a whirl of vague speculations. Thirsting for knowledge, as yet he advances slow and fumbling toward his destiny. But already, the thoughtful, introspective life has given him a sense of inner dignity. Thinking of great things, his manner has acquired a touch of greatness. The sea and his ambitions have given him his first patent of nobility.

How much more remarkable, for a man of his condition, was this courage of the soul than the trivial daredeviltries which he later invented to ornament this period of his life. It would have been about this time, according to these legends, that he took part in a desperate naval engagement, off Cape Vincent, in which more than twenty ships engaged. Don Fernando, in the *Historie*, describes the encounter, placing his father in the fleet of the commander known as the Admiral Coullon, nicknamed *Columbus Archipyrata*.

There were two sea-rovers who bore the peaceful name of "dove." One, Georges Paléologue, called Bissipat, was a member of an ancient family, descending from the Emperors of Byzance. He chose the title of *Columbus Pyrata*. The other, *Columbus Archipyrata*—the "arch-piratical dove"—was the younger son of a Gascon family, a great captain and a formidable fighter. He rose to be a Vice-Admiral of France, as Garnier relates in his *Histoire de France*, "and was known by the name of Admiral Coullon, and feared as such in all the seas".

Coullon, Coulon or Coulomb is merely the French approximation of the Latin, Columbus, and it is with this renowned personage that Christopher claimed relation. It is extremely likely, however, that he had no idea of the man's lineage or position. The Vice-Admiral's real name was Guillaume de Casenove, an entire ignorance of which fact, both on the part of Christopher and Fernando, renders their claim to kinship rather trivial.

There was, however, a battle. The truth apparently is that Christopher was engaged on the side opposed to his pretended namesake, and came off the worse for it, in consequence.

In the year 1476, his employers, Spinola, di Negro and Squarciafico, commissioned a fleet of merchant vessels for a voyage to England. Again, the name of Columbus is missing from the list of the crew; his post, then, was once more that of supercargo. The fleet sailed from the harbor of Noli, carrying goods of unusual value; one ship alone, the Bechella, had a cargo rated at one hundred and fifty thousand ducats.

Naturally, such a prize could not escape the watchful eyes of the corsairs. The thirteenth of August, as the convoy was abreast the Cape of Saint Vincent, Coullon, at the head of twelve ships-of-the-line and five lighter vessels, attacked. The battle lasted ten hours, with little advantage to either side. Then, fearing the outcome, Coullon resorted to the use of incendiary bombs. Three of the Genoese vessels burst into flames, but the fire spread to the decks of the French ships, with which they were close grappled, and all sank, burning.

Some Portuguese schooners, running out from Lagos to watch the battle, succeeded in saving a hundred men. The Botinella, under Antonio di Negro, and one of the Spinola's galleys escaped, limped into Cadiz and, from there, made their way to Lisbon. As for Columbus, Fernando relates that "being a good swimmer, and finding himself at the distance of two leagues from the land, he seized an oar, and by its aid succeeded in reaching the shore. Whereupon, learning that he was not far from Lisbon, where he knew he should find many natives of Genoa, he went thither, and meeting with a gratifying reception, took up his abode in that city."

Whether, on his first visit to the Portuguese capital, he arrived in so dramatic a fashion, or came in on one of the boats, is not of great importance. He did not remain long. Before Fall, a new fleet sent out from Genoa under Paolo di Negro, Matteo d'Oria, and Benedetto Italiano made port at Lisbon, re-embarked the cargo and survivors, and set sail for England.

Genoa, at that time, had its agencies in many of the British ports. A brisk commerce with the Scotch was maintained by several of the powerful Genoese families, such as the Centurione, one of whom, stationed at Lisbon, had even been nicknamed "Scoto." The fleet called at Bristol and at some of the Scottish ports, delivering merchandise billed to the agent of Luigi Centurione Scoto. They then headed northward, into the ocean.

There were good reasons for this excursion toward the fringes of the Arctic. In those days, there were large and thriving colonies established in Iceland and on the southern shores of Greenland. The schooners of the Norsemen thronged the seas, daring not only the voyage to the islands, but venturing beyond, so that even so early as the eleventh century they had touched the shores of a great new continent in the west and left colonists there.

They called it *Vinland,* and the name confuses. No undisputed trace of these earliest American colonists has yet been found, and opinion divides as to the derivation of the name. Their landing has been conjectured as far south as New York. Others pretend that they entered the Gulf of the Saint Laurence, where Cartier later saw "great store of the wild grape, covered with bloom." On the other hand, the fact that in the old Norse dialect, the word *vin* might correspond with the term for "pasture" leads some to assume that their landing was on the grassy shores of Labrador.

But by the advent of the Middle Ages, this short-lived settlement had fallen into silence. Four centuries later, Greenland itself was near being swept into oblivion, as the glacial field, moving down from the north, slowly transformed the Green Isle into a desert of ice.

During her brief prosperity, however, these islanders had maintained a brisk trade with Europe. Even in this intemperate climate, the instinct of human vanity asserted itself, and the Greenlanders dressed in the latest fashion, brought them by the Genoese traders, in return for their seal skins and musk-ox oils. And though now only their tombs remain, it is curious, on opening them, to find the bodies, in that faraway place, garbed in the elegant raiment of the fifteenth century dandy.

Columbus, in a letter quoted by Fernando, mentions this voyage, and some of his observations. Iceland was then called *Thule,* and he relates that, in the year 1477, he had "sailed one hundred leagues beyond the island of

Thule, the southern part of which is distant from the equinoctial line 73 degrees and not 63, as some assert: neither does it lie within the line which includes the west of Ptolemy, but is even more westerly. . . . At the time I was there the sea was not frozen, but the tides were so great as to rise and fall 26 fathoms. . . ."

It would be strange, if one so eager for knowledge of the world's extent, had not heard tales, in those northern ports, of the hardy ancients, and the exploits of Bjarn, and Leif, son of Eric the Red, who had gone still farther into the west, and found the sea's limits.

On the return, the Genoese galleys touched once more at Lisbon, and here Christopher signed off and landed. The voyage had taught him much of the sea and the sea's mystery, but all this, as yet, and his budding projects and conjectures as well, he kept hidden beneath the prudent reticence of the Genoan. The year was 1477.

III. THE JUDGMENT CHAIR
OF THE CENTURIONE

Lisbon was the central meeting place for sailors and cosmographers. The King, Alfonso V, called Alfonso the African, as well as his successor, King John II, encouraged with all possible enthusiasm the exploration of Africa. The Infante, Don Henriquez, nicknamed "The Navigator," himself had followed the shore of the continent as far as Cape Verde.

The Island of Santiago, just off the promontory, was supposed to contain a marvellous substance—none other than a remedy for leprosy, that malady which dismayed all Europe during the Middle Ages, Portugal alone was not to be proprietary to this cure. Louis XI of France commissioned Georges Bissipat, already known to us as *Columbus Pyrata* and now become Vicomte d'Auge et de Falaise, to explore "the Green Isle and the States of Barbarie—*l'Isle Vert et Pays de Barbarie*"—and bring back

40

a supply of the great tortoises from which the remedy was derived.

"For by eating of these tortoises," [1] writes Eustache de La Fosse, good townsman of Tournay, who visited Africa about the year 1480, "the leper may be cured, and by anointing himself with their blood and the lard of their flesh, and with this ointment seasoning all his victuals, by these means after two years' time they find themselves utterly cleansed and cured of their leprosy."

There were others of these African islands giving products less magical, but more practical in their uses. Madeira, that tree-crowned cliff of basalt, supplied Portugal with cane-sugar; besides, with the Azores and the Canaries, it made a link in the chain of harbors which protected the commerce of the kingdom with Africa.

All these islands of the littoral—and they were many—belonged, by the custom of "finders keepers" then obtaining, to their discoverers. But the world was coming to believe that beyond the waste of sea, the horizon hid countries of unsuspected immensity, whose discovery would dwarf these tiny archipelagos into insignificance.

Even in remote antiquity men's minds had speculated

---

[1] *Desquelles tortues, le ladre se guérit en les mangeant et se oingdant du sang et de la grasse à assaulcer ses viandes et par ainsi au bout de deux anz ilz se trouvent bien purgéz et guériz de leur lèpre.*

on these areas. Thus had been born the legend of Atlantis, that mighty island, believed to be wider than Asia and Africa combined. It lay somewhere beyond the Pillars of Hercules, and belonged to Poseidon, God of the Waters, being the share allotted him when the gods divided the universe between them.

And even beyond Atlantis, according to tradition, other islands were to be found. If one might find his way, the explorer could use them as stepping stones, across the ocean void, and reach the continent which lay beyond. To be sure, Plato—after a mouth-watering description of the wealth of this empire: its mighty cities, ornamented with heroic effigies of Poseidon, of the Kings of Atlantis, of the Hundred Nereids—had told how a frightful deluge had overwhelmed it all, drowning island, population and treasures together under the seas. Still, from generation to generation, the story had persisted and the treasures of Atlantis, first forged, perhaps, in the mind of some Egyptian priest, remained throughout the centuries, the glittering arcanum of man's most desire.

And there were other tales. Thus when, far out at sea, the sailors saw a flock of birds in lonely flight across the sky, they would say that these were messengers from the Enchanted Isles, a supposition that had its origin in the mass of legend surrounding the epoch of Charlemagne. For it had been in those turbulent times, when the Saracens were over-running Spain, burning and pillaging, that a good bishop of Portugal had sought refuge in these islands.

"And then this same Bishop, being of clerkly training, and skilled in the arts of magic", [2] we are told by Eustache de La Fosse, "he cast an enchantment over the islands, so that never again would they be visible to the eye of any man until the day when all the Spanish kingdoms should be restored within the good Catholic faith. And often the sailors who sail in these regions see birds flying from these islands, but never do they see any trace of the islands themselves, by reason of this same enchantment."

This was the legend of the Antilles, or *Antilia*, where gold was so plentiful that the unseen habitants used the grains for scouring their cooking pots. Beyond lay another phantom kingdom, the country of *Brésil*, source of the sweet-smelling woods whose fragments sometimes washed against the Irish shores. Salvaging this valuable flotsam was the delight of princes. Among others, Charles V of France had his reading-room in the Louvre paneled with the fragrant wood.

[2] *Et lors ledit évesque qui estoit grand clerc, sçavant l'art de nigromance, ençanta les dites isles et que jamais n'apparestroient à personne tant que touttes les Espaignes ne seroient remises à nostre bonne foy catholicque. Souvent les marinniers voioient les oiseaux de ladite isle en naviguant en iceluy quartier sans jamais pouvoir veoir rien des dictes isles, ad cause du dit enchant.*

No one, however, had yet been able to reach this land of aromatic forests, not even that Thomas Lloyd of Bristol who, it is recorded, spent nine months in their search. But year by year trade spread and the sea-paths widened, and men whose names even history has forgotten pushed out, each a step beyond the other, toward the unknown.

A passion for discovery had taken hold of the world. As the "Mississippi" gripped France under the Regency, as the Second Empire gambled in stocks at the Bourse, so now exploration was the golden bubble which all the world was bent on capturing. Princes and traders, some for pleasure and all for wealth, bought ships and sent them forth, much as today the wealthy sportsman sends his thoroughbreds to the track, and in like manner, with solemn optimism, often gave away their winnings before the race had begun.

Thus, in 1475, by gift of King Alfonso V of Portugal, one Fernao Tellez before his vessel left harbor found himself regent of all lands which he might discover in the ocean of the Atlantic—"including the Seven Cities." And again in 1486 (title lapsed quickly then) King John II invests Fernam d'Ulmo, by letters-patent, with "the large island, islands of continent lying beyond our shores and known as the Island of the Seven Cities"—on condition that the explorer, already appointed Captain of the Island of Terceire, conduct the discovery at his own expense.

Before the voyage of d'Ulmo began he had, by contract signed and sealed, ceded half his profits to another native of Madeira, Alfonso de Estreito, on the latter's engaging to furnish and outfit four caravels for the fleet. A German nobleman also joined forces with the expedition, none other than the famous cosmographer of Nüremberg, Martin Behaim, then living in Portugal and married to the daughter of the Fleming, Job van Herter, Governor of the Island of Fayal.

The projects of Behaim went far beyond the Seven Cities. He planned to reach the Indies by the western route. Though he was fated never to realize his dream, he was a leading spirit in the geographic speculation of the day. A globe, engraved by him in 1492, summarizes the theory of the period, showing the Indies, surrounded by the 12,700 islands enumerated by Marco Polo, facing Africa across the narrow ocean. Of these islands, the largest was also the richest—Cypango, clothed with pepper forests, stored with the riches of the world.

Among this fantastic horde of Portuguese adventurers moved the shrewd Genoese traders. They furnished vessels for the voyages; they chaffered over supplies. But beyond all this, their eyes were fixed steadily on the main motive of the affair—the supply of gold.

There was a dearth of the metal. Europe derived her bullion from mines which the Romans had discovered, in

Transylvania, Hungary, Bohemia, the Tyrol and Granada. And the production of these workings combined gave an annual total of only one hundred and eighty kilograms, less than 397 pounds—actually not enough to meet the loss which, through abrasion or from "clipping," the coined gold suffered every year! In the fifteenth century, the massed gold supply of Christendom—coined or otherwise—did not exceed $12,000,000. And each year saw this meager hoard diminishing, as greater purchases of spices, silks, and jewelry entailed heavier shipment of gold in payment to the Orient. Here was a financial crisis with a vengeance!

The Hundred Years' War, moreover, had upset still further the financial system of the continent. The *livre tournois*—the goldpiece of Tours, struck by the Crown of France and the standard coin of the period—declined to one-tenth its value, and in the general depreciation of currency all the great trading centers were hard shaken—of these none more so than Genoa, greatest of them all.

An association of financiers at that city, hastily met, promised to combat the crisis, stabilizing the florin at 44 sols, if they were given the monopoly of coinage for a period of five years. The Government refused. It was then that Benedetto Centurione, one of the Directors of the Banca di San Giorgio urged the government to put its coinage on a gold basis.

Thus, Benedetto's proposal stated, "The banks would be forced to pay in gold florins; the florin would be the basis of money changing, and thus the gold supply would remain in the country, driving out money of baser coinage and becoming, in time, the basis of the nation's wealth."

His plan was adopted. Next year, the Council decreed that all bills drawn against Genoa, or in her favor, must be made payable in gold. The net result was to spur on the Genoese trader in the hunt for gold. The decree limited his transactions to the amount for which he could offer payment in gold. Obviously, then, the man who could discover new deposits of the ore would wield a power in the city's commerce more valuable even than the metal he might obtain.

Among the Ligurian merchants, the Centurione were regarded as being, if not the wealthiest, certainly the most enterprising. Their branches and agencies were everywhere. Carlo Centurione went to Brussels to represent the family—with the King's own seal for safe-conduct across France. Teramo headed the agency at Cadiz. Martino conducted affairs in Granada, with Niccolo Centurione in Majorca and Paolocelle at Lisbon. They had representatives at Constantinople and at Trebizond.

Despite this, the Turkish onslaught had seriously crippled their affairs in the Orient. Successively, passage through Mesopotamia, then the Euxine Pont and the Caspian had been blocked or rendered difficult. Toward the end of the century, one of the family was dispatched to Moscow, hoping to persuade the Grand Duke to open a new commercial route through the Baltic into Asia. Nowhere perhaps, could the current of world affairs be better watched and measured than from the offices in the *Contrada San Siro* at Genoa where the modest old family device of the Centurione—the *scagno, scanno*: "the bench"— marked the headquarters of the great trading house.

Here could be seen Messer Lodisio Centurione, head of the home office, bending his head to scan the reports and check the sums of the day's trading. A cloth of Saracen weaving, perhaps, is folded across his desk. The shelves that surround him are filled with papers, neatly arranged. Near at hand stand the seals and stamps, a goldsmith's scales, an incense-burner of Damascene workmanship. Everything is ordered, arranged; the old head under the furred hood moves slowly up and down as the lists are scanned and the totals tallied. Method, detail, calm— but the mind behind it all looks out to the world's rim, where the ships come and go with his cargoes.

For the moment, the eye of this great trader was bent on Africa, where the Portuguese explorations had opened the way for a profitable traffic in gold dust, sugar, and slaves. King John II of Portugal, claimed the monopoly of this trade and had so far succeeded in maintaining it, as Eustache de La Fosse, who tried to smuggle through the Portuguese controls, had learned to his sorrow.

The Genoese, however, by agreement with King John, had a share in the African trade. So far, only the islands and the coastal regions had been exploited. But men pushed on, hoping in time to penetrate to the center of the continent where, according to report, lay the realm of a Christian King—Prester John. And he, it was hoped, would aid them on, along the rest of the way to the Indies, land of spice and gold.

From his desk in the *Contrada San Siro,* Lodisio Centurione watched the advance of commerce and the progress of navigation toward these ends. And while the explorers pushed on toward Africa's core, he continued to ship out textiles and import the native products.

Thus, in July, 1478, he enters a combination with Paolo di Negro, stationed at Lisbon, to buy sugar at Madeira. Christopher Columbus is put in charge of the expedition, and sails for the islands. But communications go astray; funds arrive too late. Columbus is able to buy only a small part of the quantity desired. And a dispute intervenes between the two financiers.

Lodisio brings suit before the Civil Courts of Genoa against the di Negro brothers, Paolo and Cazano. According to his complaint, he had authorized them to advance the sum of 1290 ducats to Christopher Columbus, for the purchase of sugar in the Island of Madeira. Instead, the brothers had given him only 103½ ducats, and an assortment of cheap merchandise for barter. Columbus had made the journey to Madeira but, through this default of the di Negro, he was unable to charge the ship with a full cargo and the voyage, consequently, resulted in loss.

Two days later, on August 25, 1479, Columbus himself was called to testify. The interrogation took place in the offices of the *Contrada San Siro*, before the famous *scagno* of the Centurione. According to Italian custom, a *notaio*, Gerolamo Ventimiglia, presided. Though the examination was conducted in Italian, the process is drawn in Latin, and witnessed by two Genoese citizens, Giovanni-Battista de Cruce, and Giacobbe Sclaniva.

After the customary preamble—"In witness for Lodisio Centurione, by the Grace of God, Amen. Be it known that in this place and in the presence of the witnesses undersigned, we have this day summoned and interrogated Christopher Columbus, citizen of Genoa (Christophorus Columbus, Civis Janue) . . ." [3]—the deposition of Columbus begins.

He states that in July of the previous year he was located

---

[3] This important document was first published by Assereto, in the *Giornale Storico e Litterario della Liguria*; Spezia, 1904, and reprinted recently by M. Charles de La Roncière: *La Découverte de l'Afrique*; Paris, 1927.

at Lisbon; that Paolo di Negro sent him to Madeira to buy 2400 arrobe (about 78,000 pounds) of sugar, providing him, however, with only 115,000 reals, increasing the sum later to 312,000 reals; that, this sum being insufficient for his purchases, the merchants of Madeira threatened to put the sugar up to auction. That, further, the owner of the vessel, one Ferdinand de Palos, demanded carrying charges for the full cargo, although they came back very light.

His answers to the formal questions reveal the shrewd, guarded character of the man. Asked his plans, he replies that he leaves tomorrow, for Lisbon.

To the question of age, fortune and opinion in the suit, he answers that he is twenty-seven years of age, has at present only one hundred florins, and desires that "he will gain judgment who has the most right on his side."

Until now, Columbus had cut little figure as a mariner; his travels were made rather as supercargo, commission buyer, or commercial representative. However, the notary's sitting in the Centurione offices had given the youth plenty of food for thought.

He had breathed the same air as the trading captain himself, and the obscurity of his own position became trebly apparent to him. And what future lay before him? Nothing but the grind and scrape of the common herd, unless. . . . Unless by some daring stroke he might outstrip them all! Suppose, for example, he could discover the

51

new route to the East, and its gold and its spices! It would be his turn then to condescend, even to the mighty Messer Lodisio himself. So he went dreaming back to Lisbon.

But in Columbus, a passion for cosmography gave his dreams a solider outline than most; his ambitions gave them purpose. And now his travels recommenced.

He who, in the great Genoese galleys, had seen Chio, Iceland, Madeira—the very limits of the known world— must now go forth in the smaller ships of the Portuguese. Lonely voyages, as super-cargo, among strangers. Lonely ashore, too, with only a few friends from Genoa in the foreign city. But loneliness breeds introspection; Columbus' mind, more and more, was haunted by the thought of what might lie beyond man's farthest travels—beyond the horizon.

His age was twenty-eight. His custom was to go to prayers at the Convent of Santos, much favored in those days as a retreat by the ladies of the Court. The sisters wore the habit of the Order of Santiago, but were constrained by no vow of celibacy; they were free to marry. Dona Anna de Mendoça, Mother-Superior of the Order, had been at one time the mistress of King John II. One of the young ladies lodged at the convent was the Dona Filepa Moniz Perestrello.

. . .

The Perestrello, native of Piacenza, in Lombardy, had come to Portugal at the close of the fourteenth century. Here a son, Bartolomeo, married Margarida Martins. Later, his first wife dying, he married Isabel Moniz de l'Argarve.

Bartolomeo was for a time gentleman-in-waiting to the person of the Infante, Dom John. At the death of King Alfonso V, and the accession of John to the throne, Perestrello became a member of the retinue of Dom Henriquez, the "Navigator."

In this capacity, he accompanied the young prince on his voyages, down the coast of Africa. On one such journey they coasted past Madeira and on to the Island of Porto-Santo, where they intended to establish a colony. They landed a troop of emigrants there, supplied them with implements and domestic animals—including a family of rabbits, which multiplied so rapidly that before long they had become a serious menace to cultivation.

However, the colony grew and prospered. Meanwhile, Perestrello was using his influence at court. His two sisters, Isabel and Branca, were both mistresses of Dom Pedro de Noronha, Archbishop of Lisbon. By their aid, in 1446, he was appointed Hereditary Captain of the isle.

So Perestrello, the graying courtier, settled at Porto-Santo. Here he strove with the rabbits, married Isabel Moniz, had three children, and died in 1457. His widow returned to Lisbon, placed Felipa at school in the Convent of Santos.

.   .   .

Christopher was tall, ruddy-cheeked, with a cleft chin and yellow hair tinged with white, and eyes whose blue was deepened by that troubled sense of yearning that strikes at women's hearts. Such a man stood out, among the dark and dancing Portuguese. Such a man would be noticed, as he knelt at prayers in the Convent of Santos.

He was noticed, by the eyes of the young Felipa Perestrello. Soon the family, proud of their Italian origin, was giving a hospitable welcome to their young compatriot. Perhaps, too, mingled with their patriotic souvenirs, was the remembrance of the family Colomb, of the nobility of Piacenza. Christopher had no concern in that. He found himself welcome in a family of lonely ladies, admired by the heiress of a famous Captain of the Islands.

What matter if the captain had been a courtier, not a sailor—no hero, but a fortunate weakling? Such questions are but the indiscretions of the historian; Christopher did not trouble himself with them. Meanwhile, there was no doubt that Isabel Moniz, wife of Perestrello and mother of Felipa, belonged to the highest strain of the Portuguese nobility. In the Genoese colony at Lisbon, whispers began to pass: Christopher was beginning to *tes-*

sersi la famiglia—"to weave himself a family"—he who had woven other cloth before!

It was a strange alliance, and a stranger bridal. The two were married toward the close of the year 1479, and though there is no doubt of the young island-girl's love for her husband, it may be questioned whether the reserved Ligurian shared her ardor. Perhaps he married, not the woman, but the dream—of wealth, of fame, which her dowry gave him the practical means to pursue.

Whether they lived, these first years, in Lisbon or on the island is not known. Certainly, Christopher visited Porto-Santo frequently; his family-in-law had large holdings there. Old Perestrello, too, dilettante sea-venturer and ruler of an important port of call, had collected a considerable library of nautical lore. Christopher used this information, combined with his central position at Madeira and Porto-Santo, to keep himself well informed of all the projects and discoveries which occupied the world of the day.

Soon, he had undertaken several voyages down the coast to the Guineas, where a curious sort of blind traffic was carried on by the Arabs.

By this system, the traders brought their merchandise to the shores and piled it there, then retired some miles away. When the natives arrived, they put a pile of gold-dust beside the goods they wanted to buy, and disappeared again, leaving the field clear for the Arabs to return. The traders weighed the gold and, if enough had been brought to pay for the goods, they took their pay and left the merchandise, and sailed away. This complicated system had obtained for centuries between the Negroes and the Arab traders, and now the Portuguese followed it in their turn. It was in this wise that most of the African gold—gold which the Christians believed to come across the continent from the Indies—was brought in.

And—"The Indies hold many things of value," Columbus noted in the margin of his volume of the *Historia rerum ubique gestarum*, by Pius II, "including aromatic spices, store of precious stones, and mountains of gold."

His spare time he devoted to reading and self-education. In this, his brother Bartholomew, now living at Lisbon, was of great assistance. Ten years younger, better educated, and well-grounded especially in the art of cosmography, Bartholomew earned his living as a mapmaker.

.   .   .

In those days, map-making was a rare and highly-valued accomplishment. In 1438, there was but one man in Genoa versed in the art, Agostino di Noli by name. He was freed of all tax-payments on his agreement to teach the craft to his brother. But charting distant places bred in the brothers a desire to visit them, and soon the di Nolis sailed to the Cape Verde Islands, leaving a priest, Bartolomeo da Pareto, to continue their work in Genoa. This craftsman was deemed so indispensable to the Republic that, in 1453, with unconscious humor, they rewarded the worthy pastor with the immunities and preferences which were given to the fathers of twelve children!

Thus a man who knew how to draw marine charts had no difficulty in earning a livelihood. But the practice of the profession entailed constant application; reports of voyages must be obtained (no easy matter in those days of slow communications), books of old travellers must be studied, captains must be interviewed—even the lowly sailors might have information. Every voyage was a voyage of discovery; the map-maker must watch the changing scene with the vigilance of a lighthouse-keeper.

Meeting Bartholomew, then, gave an added spur to Christopher's eagerness. The two brothers went ardently to work, reading and analyzing books and manuscripts, filling margins with their annotations, written in scripts as similar as their ideas, and as precise.

Among the books (all annotated) preserved by his son, Fernando, were: the *Historia rerum ubique gestarum*, by Pope Pius II, printed at Venice in 1477 and in Columbus' possession by the year 1481; a Latin translation of Marco Polo; an Italian translation of Pliny's Natural History, from the press of Zani de Portesio at Venice, 1489; the

Lives of Plutarch, translated into the Castilian by Alonso de Paleneia, and printed at Seville in 1491. The notations reveal that Christopher might have made some pretension as a linguist: they vary from Portuguese to Castilian, to Italian and, most often, to Latin.

Most important to his mental development was, undoubtedly, the *Imago Mundi*, of Pierre d'Ailly, Bishop of Cambrai. This Churchman, whom his contemporaries called "The Eagle of France," came to his bishopric in 1411 and died in 1420, having published poems, sermons and works on cosmography. No traveller, his attempts in world-study were purely theoretical, and are based on the speculations of Aristotle, Pliny, and Roger Bacon. His *Imago Mundi*, of which Christopher possessed a copy, was printed at Louvain by Jean de Westphalie in 1483. It was Columbus' most treasured text. "D'Ailly, among the old writers," says Las Casas, "is certainly the one who inspired in Columbus the most confidence in his projects."

Columbus' copy is now preserved in the *Bibliotheca Colombina* at Seville. The margins contain more than eight hundred notations, in Latin. In many places, passages of particular interest are underscored; many of his notes are marked by the sign of the cross. In general, he seems most to have been interested in the learned Bishop's conclusions concerning the smallness of the globe and the necessarily short distance between Spain and the Indies, if one travelled across the Atlantic.

Thus, on the back of the forty-second page, we find the following notation: *Mare Rubrum est six menses navigationis et de ibi annum usque ad Indiam unde Salomis per triennium deportabat commertia*—"To cross the Red Sea requires six months' sailing, and from there, a year more is needed to reach the Indies. Thus the commerce of Solomon required three years for a voyage."

These three notes we have quoted sum up roughly the conclusions which Columbus drew from his studies, in books which he venerated as the oracle. One: that Asia was the land of gold. Two: that the way by the East was long. Three: that to the westward only a narrow sea separated him from all this wealth.

Obviously, beside the knowledge of true scientists, even of that day, Columbus' theories seem weak indeed. But, in him, too much learning would have confused him. He needed only enough to give play to those qualities of observation, gregariousness, perseverance and initiative which were his chief strength.

So he thumbs his maps, and cross-questions sailors on their adventures, and comes home with armsfull of beach-combings, to study what the tides have washed in. Sometimes he salvages a bit of wood, carved in strange pattern, sometimes a branch of an unknown shrub, or a thick-

AN ENGRAVING FROM THE COSMOGRAPHIA,
OF MUNSTER.

"Sailing ships, hardly larger than a Banks fisherman today, ranged through the Mediterranean. . . .
But beyond this little circle stretched the great dark
waste which the Mariners called the 'Ocean-Sea,'
remote and unapproachable as the stars, swimming
with monsters, filled with terror, breathing of death."

jointed strip of bamboo, sometimes a piece of dark timber, from which the salt has not yet driven all trace of its exotic odor. Sometimes he stumbles on a corpse tumbled up by the waves, and is struck by the strange horror in the eyes.

With all his studies, the stronger his conviction grew that the land of his desire lay west, beyond the sea. He was not alone in this conviction; in fact, there were those among the more imaginative of his contemporaries who had dreamed so much of these western lands that they believed they had seen them. Fernam Domingo de Arco, a native of Madeira, obtained in 1484 the grant of this phantom shore from King John II, but was never able to set foot there. And the Fleming, Antonio Leme, with the same pretensions, met the same fate.

Hundreds of others were occupied with the same ideas as Columbus. Everywhere—in England, as well as among the Mediterranean nations, and in Normandy—men's eyes were turned to the sea. Dieppe, at that time the principal harbor of France, was noted for its fearless sailors. In 1365, they had sailed beyond Cape Verde, and had established a colony, naming it *Petit-Dieppe*, in the section which the Portuguese later called *Sierra-Leone*. But after 1410, France, weakened by her civil wars, could not keep up her commerce with Africa. The Portuguese replaced the Norman colonists. And though, in 1402, a Norman noble, Jean de Bethancourt, Chamberlain to Charles VI, conquered the Canaries and assumed their government, he died in 1425. When, under Louis XI, France was strong again, the Portuguese had made themselves masters of the African coast.

With Africa closed to them, the mariners of Dieppe looked for other fields to conquer. In 1488, a group of merchants commissioned a vessel under the command of one Captain Cousin who, breaking with the custom of coastal exploration, set his prow for the open sea.

After two months' sailing, he landed on the shore of what later Norman students were to maintain to have been South America. Whether truly so or not—and no possible proof is available—the important thing is that Cousin did nothing to develop his discovery.

From then on, voyages from Dieppe were undertaken by individual traders who, through professional jealousy, concealed both the aims and the success of their journeyings. When, in 1694, the Town Hall of Dieppe was bombarded and destroyed by the English, all trace of these early voyages was destroyed in the burning of the City's archives.

Nevertheless, some rumor of these travels reached the outside world. Dieppe was a harbor and supply station for the Italian ships, on their trading trips with the North, and the vessels of Dieppe themselves carried usually on long journeys a Spanish or Portuguese interpreter in their complement. Thus the news of their ventures filtered through Europe, spurring on the other nations.

Still more exciting were the enterprises which the Danish sailors undertook, at the instigation and perhaps with the coöperation of the Portuguese. Since Henry the Navigator, Portugal had been constantly striving to break through the Infidel line and reach the realm of Prester John, reputed Christian ruler of the Indies.

The obstacles to the southern route appearing insurmountable, they turned to the North, enlisting the aid of the Danes. At first, the Danish sailors did no more than accompany the royal Henry on his travels. Later, in 1476, the King of Denmark himself equipped a fleet which, sailing for the Indies, ended by discovering Labrador.

At all events, a globe engraved in 1537 by the mathematician Gemma Frisius, and the cartographer Gerhard Mercator, now preserved at Zerbst, bears across the Arctic regions of North America, the inscription: "Arctic strait, or Strait of the Three Brothers, by which the Portuguese attempted to sail to the Orient, the Indies, and Molucca."

And lower, at the region of Labrador: "Here live the races whom Joannes Scolvus, the Dane, visited around the year 1476."

•　　•　　•

Though many of these voyages accomplished little, they prove how filled was the world with the passion for discovery. Tales without number of the great voyages went from mouth to mouth, from nation to nation. To the young Columbus, they were like a ferment in his soul. And from one of these voyages he was to draw a more practical benefit.

Some time before, a Portuguese vessel sailed with a cargo of merchandise for Flanders. Some days out, contrary winds arose. The ship was driven from its course; the gale became a tempest; they could do nothing but run for it. So, for days on end, they scudded westward and still westward, into unknown waters, and finally to the shore of an unknown island.

The return was more terrible than the voyage out. Provisionless, waterless, more than half died of privation on the way. The others dropped anchor at last, to die, in Madeira. Columbus offered to take the only survivor into his home, at Porto-Santo. The man was a pilot, a one-eyed Galician. It has been said that he was an old friend of Columbus, though it is perhaps more likely that Christopher's hospitality grew out of his interest in the man's adventures. In any case, his charity was well repaid for before his death, the old sailor had given him a full account of the voyage, as well as an exact description of the island they had discovered.

Sixteenth century authors make much of this dying revelation, and though—since men hear best what they want to hear, and the speaker is apt to pander to this desire—it is possible that the fever-haunted old sea-dog may have found much inspiration in the eager questioning of his host, it is certain that Columbus himself found all his theories confirmed and his hopes magnified by the deathbed confession. He was now to receive the testimony on the same subject of a man of world-famed erudition: the Doctor Paolo Toscanelli.

A Florentine, his fame was so great that in 1458, the Portuguese ambassadors to the Council of Mantua paid a special visit to him, for instruction in cosmography. According to the custom of the times, he maintained correspondents in the different capitals of Europe, whose reports, coupled with the chance reports of travellers, constituted the sole means of following the course of international ideas.

In 1474, the Canon Fernam Martins wrote him on behalf of the King of Portugal, to ask his opinion on the possibility of reaching the Indies from the West. Toscanelli hastened to reply to the royal query, and enclosed, with his letter dated June 25, 1474, a nautical chart.

Now, the Perestrello were related to the Martins, and in this way, Christopher heard of this latest correspondence on his favorite subject. He, too, addressed himself to

Toscanelli. Lorenzo Girardo [4] a Florentine merchant, established at Lisbon, undertook the delivery of the letter.

. . .

Paolo del Pozzo Toscanelli—Paulus Tuscus to the students, Maestro Pagolo to his friends—was born in 1397. The son of a Florentine Doctor of Medicine, he entered in 1425 the corporation of the *Medici e speziali*—the Doctors and Apothecaries. A patrician, and of a family which had grown wealthy in agriculture and in trade, Maestro Pagolo preferred the sciences. He excelled as much by his character as by his learning, and made an important member of the learned group which frequented the bookshop owned by Vespasiano da Bisticci.

In those days, at Florence, the book-shops and their owners populated the *via degli Librai*—the Street of Bookshops—now the *via della Condotta*. Their shops were the meeting-places where gathered the men of letters, the students, the distinguished visitors of the day.

Vespasiano, leader among these caterers to the learned, had earned the title of "Prince of Librarians." At about the year 1480 he retired, taking a retreat in the countryside near Antella where, by his own account, "could be found neither women nor mosquitoes, nor any other enemy of sleep."

[4] or Briardo.

Here, in his solitude, the aging bookworm remembered his famous customers and cronies, now scattered from Oxford to Budapest, from Germany to the Sicilian Isles. He determined to write their biographies. And in his book—naïve as compared to the Humanists of the day, but for that the more vivid—the whole literary life of the Renaissance lives again. His description of the patriarch Toscanelli, to whom Giraldi was to present Christopher's letter, is among the most curious:

"Maestro Pagolo, son of the worthy Doctor Dominico, Florentine, was a descendant of a most honorable family. He was greatly learned in Greek and in Latin, as well as in the seven liberal arts, which he began to study in his very infancy; but among the many sciences which he studied, he excelled chiefly in astrology, in which he was more learned than any of his fellows.

"He kept his accomplishments well hid, never boasting, never proffering his opinions; but when a friend came to him, Maestro Pagolo, especially if it were a question concerning his favorite study, was always willing with his aid. He joined to these extraordinary accomplishments a remarkable purity of living. There were many who believed him to be a virgin; for many years he slept, fully clothed, on a board settle placed beside his work-desk. He ate no meat, or nearly none, nourishing himself with fruits and vegetables, which he washed down with fresh water. He never wore a fur-trimmed bonnet in his life, but a woven one, all winter.

"By nature taciturn, he listened much and spoke seldom. His nature was so gentle, his speech and character so pure that he could not hear a profane word without showing by his whole expression his disgust.

"He was pious, and faithful to the church. He loved the good, and the faithful, who loved and feared God.

"Beside his skill in astrology, he was a remarkable geometrician. On friendly terms with the learned men of his day, he was in constant relations with them, but with none more closely than with Nicolao Nicoli, who loved and respected him, as did Ser Filipo di ser Ugolino (Brunelleschi), Lionardo d'Arezzo, frate Ambrogio, maestro Gianozzo Manetti. All these loved him much, and he discoursed much with them. He was welcome, too, in the palace of Cosimo de Medicis, who loved and respected him. Maestro Pagolo had no interest in money; his whole interest lay in honor and accomplishment, and all his glory was there. . . .

"When he was not occupied with his studies, he would visit friends who were sick; beyond this, he seldom practiced in medicine. The rest of his time was passed in the company of the famous men whose names I have mentioned. He was never heard to speak ill of any one.

Maestro Pagolo was very wise in all things; when he visited anyone who was sick, he insisted that he be confessed, and unless this was done, he would visit him no more. So he lived in saintly abstinence, fasting, sleeping on his bench, never tasting wine, and thus he lived over eighty years, and died holily, with his last breath commending himself to God in devotion and humility."

We may add that, like most of the Florentines, the austere doctor kept throughout life a sincere love of nature. He lived much in the country, and retained the freshness of outlook which such a life inspires. In addition to his estates, he owned an interest in the famous copper mines of Montecatini. His nephews were in the spice trade, in the Orient.

Columbus' letter, then, could not have fallen into better hands than those of this savant, whose fame had not clouded his interest in other men's ideas, nor cooled his enthusiasm for research. Moreover, it pleased him to discover that his unknown compatriot at Lisbon was working on a problem in which he himself was deeply interested. He welcomed the young man's appeal, and hastened to forward him a copy of the letter which he had sent to the King, inclosing with it a chart drawn by his own hands.

The original of this letter is lost. There remains, however, a copy, written either by Christopher or Bartholomew, on a cover page of the *Historia rerum ubique gestarum*:

"To Christopher Columbus; Paul, Doctor, Greetings:

"I learn of your great and magnificent desire to discover the way to the land of spices and in answer to your letter I send you a copy of another letter which some time ago I wrote to a friend and intimate of the Most Serene King of Portugal, before the wars of Castille, in answer to a letter which, by order of His Highness, he had written me on the same question; and I also send you a marine chart similar to the one which I sent to him. A chart which will satisfy your needs; the copy of the letter is as follows:

"Paul, Doctor, to Fernam Martins, Canon at Lisbon, Greetings:

"I was pleased to learn that you are in good health, and to learn that you are favored with the friendship of your King, who is a most generous and mighty prince.

"Since I talked to you some time ago of a route to the land of spices, by way of the sea, and shorter than the passage you are searching along the coast of the Guineas, your Most Serene King now asks me for an explanation of this route, or rather a plan for the eyes to see, and so clearly that even an unlearned sailor might find this route and follow it with understanding.

70

"For myself, although I know that this chart could best be made in form, like that of the world, of a sphere, I have nevertheless decided, for greater clearness and ease, to draw it up in the way used to make marine charts.

"I am, then, sending to His Majesty a chart made by my hand, upon which are shown your shores and islands from which you will depart, heading westward unchangingly; also the countries to which you should attain; likewise the distances you should keep, both from the Pole and from the Equinoctial Line, and in what direction, that is to say: within how many miles you should arrive in those lands which are richest in spices and precious stones.

"And be not surprised that I call them 'occidental,' these lands of spice, although commonly they are called 'oriental.' For to those who go by sea and by way of the interior hemisphere, these lands will lie always to the West; while he who goes by land and by way of the upper hemisphere will have them always to the East.

"Furthermore, the vertical lines drawn with relation to the height of the chart, will mark the distances from the West to the East; while the transverse lines mark the space which extends from the South to the North.

"I have also marked on the chart many other distant places to which you might come; and I have done this for the greater information of those who will make the voyage, in case the winds or some accident should drive them

71

elsewhere than where they intended—and also that they may show the natives of these lands that they know something of the country, which should please them.

"It is said that there are no other professions in these islands than that of the merchant, and, truly, there are so many sea captains and traders there that the one great part of Zaiton alone contains more than all our known world; and it is said that each year one hundred great ships loaded with pepper enter the port, without counting the other ships which bring in other spices.

"The country is populous, and rich in a number of provinces, principalities, kingdoms, and cities without number, the whole under the rule of one sovereign, called the 'Grand Kan,' signifying in Latin the King of Kings—*Rex Regum*. For the most part of the time, the siege and residence of this prince is in the province of Catay.

"His ancestors showed a disposition to come to terms with the Christians. Two hundred years ago, they sent deputies to the Pope, asking that men skilled in religious doctrine be sent to them, for they were anxious to enter into the Faith. But those who were sent encountered so many difficulties on the way that they turned back, and never reached their destination.

"Again, in the time of Pope Eugene IV, there came to Rome an envoy who showed great interest in Christianity. I myself held long conversation with him, talking of many things, as the great size of their royal palaces, and the enormous width and length of their rivers, and the multitude of cities on each, so that, in the course of one river, there are more than two hundred cities built and fortified, with marble bridges very wide and long, and ornamented with marble columns on each side.

"It is very fitting that we Latins should search out this land, not only for the great profit that would result in gold, in silver, in precious stones of all kinds and in spices which never yet had been brought into our countries, but also because of the learned men, and the philosophers and skilled astrologers to be found there, and who by their genius and their wisdom govern all that mighty province, even to directing its armies.

"And thus much to give what satisfaction to your demands as is permitted by the press of time and the exigencies of my occupations, and full ready for what other service His Majesty may require. Done at Florence, the 25 June, 1474."

"Due west from the City of Lisbon, the chart shows 26 spaces, each one measuring 250 miles, to the noble and great City of Quinsay. The city is 100 miles in circuit, and possesses ten bridges. Its name signifies 'City of the Sky.' Great marvel is told of the number of its workshops and the wealth of its revenues. (It holds sway over almost

73

one-third of the earth's surface.) This city lies in the Province of Mangi, which adjoins the Province of Katay, where resides the King of all these lands.

"But from the Island of the Antilles, which is familiar to you, there are ten spaces to the famous Island of Cypangu. This island is very rich in gold and pearls and in precious stones, so that there the temples and royal palaces are all covered over with massy gold.

"And thus the breadth of sea to be crossed, through unknown areas, is not very great. There are many things, perhaps, which I ought to have explained more clearly, but careful study of what I have given should make the rest easy to understand.

"My best wishes to you, my very dear friend."

The authenticity of this letter has been much disputed. It has been objected that Columbus would surely have already seen the original letter sent to the King in 1474, and that, further, the advanced age of Toscanelli made it most unlikely that he would have given himself so much trouble at the behest of a stranger. These objections seem hardly tenable. It has never been customary for a person so unimportant as Christopher Columbus then was, to have access to his sovereign's correspondence, especially on so serious a subject as the discovery of the West. And certainly age, even so advanced as that of Maestro Pagolo, would not quite preclude the possibility of a generous gesture toward a brother theorist.

It may, nevertheless, seem odd to us that a great philosopher should be so willing to lay bare the results of his studies to so obscure a petitioner. But we must not judge those earlier days by the motives of our own. There are book-shops still on the street that Toscanelli frequented, but the old community of sentiment no longer animates them. The specialist of today hugs his problems to himself, but in those days when wisdom had barely begun to be formalized there was no one who might not learn from another and nowhere more than in Italy was this humility of mind more evident. It was perhaps not entirely by chance that a Genoese and a Florentine were to be the first to reach the shores of the New World. There is a measure of credit still to be bestowed on such men as Toscanelli, and the civilization they created.

To Columbus, the encouragement and advice of the venerable Florentine marked a decided step in advance. The reasoning of the scholar had confirmed the conclusion of the practical man of action. It remained now to prove the theory in reality.

John II of Portgual was a proud King. Death was the measure of those who ran counter to his will, and there had been times when his own hand had executed the sentence. But he had the name of a wise king too, open of mind, and with an interest especially set on the advancement of his country's colonial interests and the advancement of its marine.

There is proof that he had already tried to profit by the information Toscanelli had sent him. Bernaldez, a Spanish chronicler of the sixteenth century, states that "many times, the Kings of Portugal had sent envoys forth on the western seas to make what discovery they could, for many men thought that by that way one might reach lands rich in gold, but never did they attain them."

And now Columbus, aided by his friends at court and recommended by his purpose, in his turn sought audience with his sovereign.

"When the speculations born of his own voyages," writes Joao de Barros, "had been confirmed by the experiences of other men, learned in the lives of ancient explorers, he came to the King John, asking that he be given ships that he might discover the western route to the Island of Cypangu."

The conditions he demanded show his assurance of success. The rank of chevalier, with the gold spur and the title of Dom Christophe Colomb, together with the prerogatives of a Grand-Admiral, Vice-Regency of the islands and continents he might discover, and the tenth of their revenue—these were to be his reward.

Notwithstanding these not altogether modest pretensions,

King John gave the project of Columbus for examination into the hands of three of his advisers: his physician, Messer Rodrigo, his almoner, the Bishop of Tangiers, and his astrologer, Messer Josepe Vizino, a Jew. These gentlemen—the same who were later to give to Vasco da Gama the chart of courses by which he eventually reached the Indies—did not share Columbus' convictions as to the proximity of Portugal to the Asiatic coast. Well they knew how, one after another, their greatest captains had failed to pierce the mystery of that ocean.

Moreover, they were already, in a sense, committed to another project. The commerce of the kingdom, as well as the policies of the King, were directed mostly toward Africa. It seemed to them more fitting that their exploration should be along that line—a policy which, by the way, was to reach its fulfilment forty years later when da Gama rounded the Cape of Good Hope and opened the way to the true Indies.

The King, then, on their advice, refused to support the wild project of this pretentious foreigner. The good fortune which had waited on Christopher ever since his arrival in Portugal now seemed at last to have abandoned him.

After his marriage, he had not withdrawn from the business world. His affairs would not seem always to have prospered; they had only served to multiply his cred-

77

itors. At any rate we find him, in his last testament, directing his son to send certain sums to various persons, and these are apparently in payment of debts long due, for he stipulates that the recipients shall not be told by whose hand they are paid. These are, Antonio Bazo, a Genoese merchant, the heirs of Luigi Centurione, and his son-in-law, as well as the heirs of Paolo di Negro, and a certain Jew, probably a money-lender, living near the Gate of the Ghetto.

The Jews of Portugal were heavily interested, financially, in the merchant marine of the country—an interest beginning, perhaps, in the fact that they were required by law to furnish an anchor and six aunes of cable free of charge, on each ship the King might equip. It is noteworthy, too, that they were in close communication with the Jews of Spain, so that, when King John, later, came to grips with the family of Bragance, Don Isaac Abravanel, the powerful financier and their supporter, had no difficulty in finding refuge in Castille.

The Centurione, as well, had agencies in both countries. There was a branch in Cadiz, and another in Granada. It is quite possible, therefor, that Christopher's creditors influenced him to leave Portugal and seek his fortunes in a country whose naval interests were quite as great. "On the seas," comments Froissart, "the Spaniards are hardy and fearless, and their navy is large and strong."

The state of Columbus' own affairs were such as to make him look favorably on the prospect of a change. His marriage had not so far been happy. Felipa had given him all that a noble wife can give to a commoner—her hand, her love, a son, a position in the world to which he could not otherwise so easily have attained—but she had not given him happiness. She died in one of the years between 1484 and 1487, and was buried at Lisbon in the Chapel of Pity in the Carmelite Convent. Columbus never spoke of her thereafter; her name is mentioned only by his son, in his will.

There is mystery here, and a suggestion of darkness about Columbus' leavetaking. Had he, perhaps, been concerned in some political intrigue? Or did he fear the debtor's cell, his father had inhabited?

Early one morning, in the year 1484—"with the utmost secrecy"— he set out for Spain, no richer than he had come, save for a son, and an ambition.

IV. CASTILLE

Bounded by the Pyrenees, the sea and the Moors, the small expanse of the Iberian peninsula was still further divided by its enmities. Castille and Leon, Aragon and Catalonia and Portugal: its provinces were separate entities all, and alive with battle, as one faced the other, or all united in the never-ending war with the Arab. The marriage of Isabella of Castille with Ferdinand of Aragon, in 1469, marked the permanent alliance of two of these kingdoms, and the first step toward the union of all.

Isabella was the daughter of a vicious father and a dissolute mother; the atmosphere of her youth was that of treachery, licentiousness and murder,—her brother's death by poison gave her her crown. In such surroundings, for her own preservation, she soon learned to be crafty and shrewd, adroit, far-seeing and self-willed. But beneath it all, she retained a purity and piety the more remarkable for her associations and her period.

This girl with a nun's face and blue-green passionate eyes showed a wilfull rebelliousness against the suitors proposed for her, and ended by marrying her cousin, Ferdinand of Aragon, who resembled her closely in appearance, save for his thick chin and the restless eye.

And Isabella was one of those who love once, and for always. This woman who would have been worthy of the most charming Prince Charming, gave her life to a man who spent his own in dissimulation and intrigue. They were allied in one respect—their religious fervor, but piety can change as often as the countryside. The background of Ferdinand lay in the dark-shaded slopes of Umbria; among the arid and rocky Sierras, his nature took on something feverish, fanatical and repellant. Isabella, whose native Castille is reminiscent of craggy castles, was of more forthright, and more gallant mold.

This feminine Crusader, however, in a day when noblemen thought it weak and womanish to write, did not despise the arts. Pietro Martire d'Anghera, Lucio Marineo, the two Geraldini and many others—Italians, and Spaniards trained in the Italian universities—were welcome advisers to her court, though Ferdinand cared little for them.

And yet, by an odd alchemy of souls, this ill-assorted pair ruled their kingdom in perfect accord. The emblem they chose was the fasces and the yoke, and they worked

to unite all Spain beneath it with something of the un-
yielding rigor of the peasant, struggling to increase his
lands.

The Crown found its two greatest adversaries in the
Moors, and in the feudal divisions which had reduced the
land almost to armed anarchy. The two Kings—for so
Spanish usage designated this union of equal sovereigns—
were too adept a pair of politicians to use their own
strength against this double foe. They set one against
the other, and the feudal barons were urged into an increasingly costly series of Crusades against the Alhambra.
It was toward such a land of strife and intrigue that Columbus had set his face.

He was, however, too thoughtful and cautious a man
to have undertaken the step without first weighing his
chances, testing his resources, and seeking introductions in
advance. He was aided in these manoeuvres by his Italian friends at Lisbon, whose agencies in Spain kept them
informed of the course of events. He had, too, enlisted
the support of friends among the Franciscan friars. The
Order, at the moment, was very powerful at the Spanish
court.

Near the port of Palos in Estramadura—famous for its
seamen—the Franciscans maintained the monastery of
Our Lady of La Rabida. In appearance it resembled many
other religious structures of the south, composing a cir-

cular chapel, surmounted by a domed spire, and surrounded by a group of white-washed buildings, their uneven roofs covered by tiles. The great pines that surrounded it looked down at the harbor, and the masts that had once held root in the same forest beside them.

The Prior, Juan Perez, had been confessor to Isabella. Now, in the leisure of the cloister, he and a monk of the order, Father Marchena, followed the study of cosmography. Their lives were as much of the sea as were those of the sailors who came to them, for confession, from the harbor below.

Whether the Father Marchena, who was a Portuguese, had already met Columbus at Lisbon, or whether the latter came with recommendations from his friends, is not clear. But it is certain that he could have sought no more valuable acquaintance than that of the monks of La Rabida, venerated alike by the mariners of Palos, and the councillors of the Court.

Columbus was well aware of the importance of their aid. He had come to gain their friendship. He succeeded completely. "And this friar," writes Oviedo de Perez, "is the one person in the world to whom Columbus confided all his secrets, and it is even said that he received a great deal of aid and assistance from the Friar, who was very skilled in the science of cosmography."

Nevertheless, the protégé of Juan Perez could not hope

overnight to gain the ear of the Kings. To reach Seville was his first step, and as he approached, its crenelated walls and the ships moored in the mouth of the Guadalquivir must have brought him memories of the city of his birth. And it was pleasant to find that his compatriots had their quarter in the city, and their street—the *calle de Genoa.*

His aim now was to find a protector, a sponsor at the Court. Juanoto Berardi, a wealthy Florentine trader, was too astonished by his proposals to act on them. Christopher next approached the Duke of Medina-Sidonia, at one time lord of the Canaries, but this great nobleman showed no inclination to finance a voyage of exploration. Another member of his family, the Duke of Medina-Cœli, showed a livelier interest. We find him, soon after, writing to the Cardinal Mendoza:

"Most Reverend Sir,

"Your Reverence may know that I have entertained for some time one Cristobal Colomo, who came by this way from Portugal, purposing to seek the King of France, his favor and aid, in a voyage to discover the Indies; and that I myself for a time had planned to defray the venture, sending him from El Puerto with three or four well-equipped caravels that I have there, for he asked no more than these. But since I perceived that such an enterprise was properly within the province of the Queen, our Sovereign, I wrote of the project from Rota to Her Highness.

She replied, bidding that he be sent on to her, which I did. . . ."

And so, on a day in January, 1486, Columbus passed through the great arch of the Gate of Almodovar and entered the ancient capital of the Caliphs, its mosques now converted into Christian churches—the city of Cordova. Through the recommendation of Juan Perez, he had immediate audience with Hernando de Talavera, confessor to the Queen, and with Alonzo de Quintanilla, Chancellor of the Exchecquer of Castille.

And then began the weary round of the antichambers, the dreary Purgatory through which must pass all those of common birth whom ambition of advancement urges to seek the rulers of the earth.

In this interregnum of doubt and delay is lost the material for the chronicles of another Saint-Simon—the rise of the Genoese adventurer at the Court of Cordova! Here was so much that was contradictory and paradoxical. Isabella and Ferdinand, young, yet already old in conquest, with a score of victories which mounted as their treasury decreased, headed a nobility whose avarice was only equalled by their courage. Here the hot, exalted ardor of the crusader was balanced by the chill cupidity of the adventurer; they killed the Moors to obtain pardon for having poisoned one another. No stranger medley of emotions ever was seen than those of these caracolling

Spanish knights, at once the sons of chivalry and the forerunners of the mercenary soldier.

Among these men of mighty will and petty passion moved the weaver's son, seeking the means to the unknown world he dreamed of.

The sense of class distinction often leaves a man at his country's borders. So Columbus, who would have walked lightly, no doubt, before a Doria or a Fregoso, had no hesitation in adopting a tone of equality with these haughty Castillian dons. His foreign birth gave him an incognito; his air of breeding served him better than a patent of nobility.

With the language he had no difficulty. Genoa was full of tutors, teachers and actors who spoke no other tongue but Spanish. Christopher had mastered it long ago. Moreover, he was a man with one obsessing purpose, and such a one can always be persuasive. And he had, too, the seaman's sense for the favoring tide and the following breeze; it helped him here, in navigating the conflicting currents of the court.

After some few months of waiting, he was at last accorded an audience with the sovereigns.

No record remains of what must have been a curious interview. Bernaldez alone mentions it in his chronicles, and then but to say that, "He explained his world-map to them, in such fashion as to arouse in them a desire to know more of these lands he spoke of."

But it could not have been so easy as that. Even today, it is difficult for the layman properly to read a map. One can imagine, then, something of Columbus' predicament as he stood before these lofty but for all that illiterate and by our standards utterly uneducated monarchs, and tried, not only to make them understand the cryptically constructed charts of the day, but also to convince them of the still more abstruse and almost heretical conclusions he had drawn from them.

Small wonder, then, that Ferdinand immediately refused all faith in the idea. There could be no common ground of understanding between a man of Columbus' mental daring, and one so shrewd and cautious as the King. Moreover, there was a question of policy to be urged against the scheme. The Spanish fleet was at present a power in the Mediterranean, and the Crown held certain prerogatives of trade in that direction. These would certainly be lost in the shuffle, if a new route were to be opened to the Indies.

Isabella, on the other hand, was interested by the project and impressed by the man,—but not so far as to commit herself immediately. The woman in her responded to the power and courage she divined in the man who knelt before her. But the prudent Queen hesitated at the

87

expense the financing of such an expedition would cause her, as well as at the damage her prestige would suffer if the enterprise should meet with failure.

It is the sometimes cruel grace of kings to deny a favor simply by never granting it. The petitioner is left to face courteous delays and polite evasions until at last of his own accord he abandons hope—leaving the royal reputation for openhandedness uncompromised by the direct and democratic "No!" This was the manner designed to deal with Columbus. His propositions were referred to a commission of scholars, headed by Hernando de Talavera.

Las Casas describes the period of delay and uncertainty which ensued then for the Genoese adventurer: "From that day on," he writes, "the struggle he faced was long and unrelenting, and more terrible perhaps than the pains of actual combat. He had to force comprehension on those who did not understand his plans and yet believed they did. He had to make patient answer to multitudes of people who knew him not, who respected him not at all, and who constantly offered him insults which wrung his soul."

These delays, always common to the Spanish temperament, had here, however, a certain justification, both in the Crown's depleted treasury, and in their preoccupation at the moment with the *Reconquista*: the war to recapture the Moorish territory. It was not until the end of Autumn that the commission met, at Salamanca. Columbus' propositions were heard, as were the opinions of certain other learned scholars. No decision, however, was made; matters drawled on as before.

Columbus returned to Cordova. From time to time, the Kings, in their largesse, sent gifts or money "to Cristobal Colomo . . . foreigner, who is busied here on certain matters of service to Their Majesties." And this uncertain dependence on another's bounty only served to increase his impatience at the delay. So he lived, forced now to economize even on his hopes, in this strange world of Spain, at once warlike and peace-loving, haughty yet gracious, courteous but cold-hearted.

His handsome face, coupled with the sensational nature of his project, and the ardor with which he defended it, won him notice, even if it did not bring him sympathy. But with familiarity this interest staled. A fête, a reception at the Palace—all the train of trivialities attendant on the court, gradually replaced him in the common mind. And as the protection and support of one after another of these gilded gentlemen turned phantom, Columbus was forced to seek elsewhere for aid. Beggary is a bitter trade, and the more so when its end is great; he followed it without faltering. His convictions were without flaw.

And now that the glamor had departed, he was alone. Save for two men—the young Diego, pensioner of the

Franciscan Hospitalers, and his brother Bartholomew, often absent at sea—he was alone, like a man in a desert, with only the great Idea for oasis, in the sandy-seated city of Cordova.

Toward the end of 1487, came a meeting that seemed the more enchanting for the former monotony. It was with the young Beatriz Enriquez de Arana.

Her parents—Pedro de Torquemada and Ana Nunez de Arana—had been of modest condition. They died when she was eighteen, leaving her little in the way of fortune. She was living in the family of some elderly relatives, when Christopher met her.

The two met, then, in that city of sun and passion, as common sufferers from friendlessness and poverty. He was a man who had an Idea for a constant, and Hunger for an occasional companion. She was a girl without friends or fortune, and at the age when the lack of the former seems worse than the latter. Early in the year 1488, Beatriz found that she was about to become a mother.

Though the morals of the day were lax, the laws were stern. The affections of these two had grown from a community of misfortune rather than of souls. In the extremity, Christopher's ambition overcame his gallantry. He wrote to the King of Portugal, seeking an invitation to return. On the twentieth of March he received a reply,

90

in which the monarch referred to him as his "favored friend," and enclosed a royal safe-conduct—"in case you might have cause to fear our police."

Columbus, however, was not to return to Portugal. The wind changed at Court, blowing him back to favor again. New gifts of money arrived from the Sovereigns, coming just as Beatriz was in child-birth. It was a son. They named this child of poverty and despair Fernando, in honor of the King.

A year more of delay and postponement, and then, on the twelfth of May, 1489, he received the command to come once more before the Kings, then at the camp of Baza.

There were reasons of policy behind all this. Some time before, two monks of the Franciscan Order in Palestine had arrived at Baza, with summary messages from the East for the Sovereigns. The Sultan of Egypt, angered by the war of extinction waged against his brothers, the Moors, had begun to plan reprisals. Unless the Spaniards laid down their arms, he himself would undertake the reduction of the Holy Lands.

Now, the Sultan was a man of exceeding importance in those days. His capital, Cairo—called Babylon by the Christians—was a great commercial center in the Eastern trade. Thus, while his power might very well overwhelm the guardians of the Holy Land, his position might also bring commercial ruin to the Mediterranean traders.

There is no doubt that the prospect of this double blow to the Christian influence in the Orient had decided the two monarchs to reconsider Columbus' plan. And he, by instinct or by statecraft, made the one move that could, above all others, appeal to them. Isabella, deeply moved by the danger that threatened the Holy Sepulcher, had already promised the Franciscans one thousand gold ducats annually for the support of their convent there, as well as a tapestry worked by her own hands. Columbus offered all the profits that might come of his discoveries, toward a new crusade.

This was not all pretension on his part. He was a man of profound religious spirit; Crusades and pilgrimages were often in his mind in later life. It is quite possible that he made his offer in the purest sincerity. Whether or no, it could not but please the pious Queen. She was unable, however, to offer him anything more than her esteem. Once more, the man who was to double the world's area found himself in Cordova, with empty pockets.

His patron and fellow-countryman, the papal legate Antonio Geraldini, was dead. Columbus was left with no other means of support save what he could earn by the sale of his maps. "Poverty," says Las Casas, "forced him to fall back on the engraving of nautical charts for his livelihood, and for this he showed great aptitude, so that he sold many to the mariners."

Nevertheless, in spite of all industry, he was often obliged to seek aid from the Franciscans. "Columbus," writes the brother of Geraldini, "deprived of all human support, betrayed by his friends, besieged by poverty, fell in such state that he was forced to go to a monastery of the Franciscan Order near the city of Marchena, as a humble suppliant begging food to sustain his very life." The Genoese had not learned, it will be seen, the vanity of those Spanish gentlemen who, though starving, would still stroll with the crowds in the plaza, picking their teeth with a bit of straw, as if they had just left the table.

And now, like the final blow to his despair, came the news that the royal commission had passed, unfavorably, on his proposition.

Hernando de Talavera, Prior of the monastery of Our Lady of the Prado, was, it will be remembered, the president of this assembly. Of the rest, the name of only one member remains—Don Rodrigo Maldonado, Councillor of the Crown and later Governor of Salamanca. The others, no doubt, were theologians, functionaries of the Crown, and perhaps some few monks who had mastered the rudiments of cosmography.

And thus their decision becomes more clearly understandable. The case was somewhat as if a commission of cabinet officers, diplomats, clergymen and police officers had been formed in, let us say, the year 1900 to consider the propositions of a man who claimed to have invented a flying machine. One can imagine the nature of their deliberations. Most of the members would immediately brand the whole thing a piece of purest folly; some might hold that the thing itself was not impossible, and a few might feel that the invention could accomplish it. But all, without doubt, would have felt that even if man could fly, it would be of small practical use to him, or to the State, and would consequently have advised the Government against investing in it. So with Talavera and his fellows.

"They held," says Las Casas, "his promises and his offers to be inacceptable and vain and impossible. . . . And in this decision they appeared before the Kings and made their report according to that opinion, persuading them that it would ill accord with the royal authority to favor a project which was built on so weak a foundation that even the most unlearned could perceive how impossible of achievement it was—since by so doing they would certainly lose what moneys they might advance toward it, and would also weaken the prestige of their royal names."

But Columbus had gone too far to draw back now. In fact, there was nowhere for him to go but onward. A return to Genoa would offer him but little encouragement. To be sure, he might submit his plans to the Centurione— but from then on, his share in their execution would only be that of an underling. How, after all, could the mighty *Officium Gazarie* be expected to put the command of one of its fleets in the hands of the son of the bankrupt weaver and pot-house keeper of the *via del Mulcento?* And in Venice, the law itself would defeat his chances: none but a nobleman of Venetian birth could head their expeditions. If he would find success, it must be farther afield.

As early as the year 1488, his brother Bartholomew had made a trip to England, in the hope of interesting King Henry VII in their project. His profession of map-engraver had prompted him to present his petition in an unusual fashion. The astonished monarch received a globe, which bore the following inscription:

"To you whose desire it is to know all the regions of the earth, this accurate portrayal will teach you what the learned know of their extent. It is drawn according as Strabo, Ptolemy, Pliny and Isidoro, in their varying fashions, described it. Here is shown as well that zone of torrid heat, unknown until recently traversed by Spanish sailors, which now many have visited.

"This in the name of the designer: of the country of Genoa, and of name, Bartholomew Columbus, this work was completed in London, in the year of Our Lord 1488, and the thirteenth day of February. In God's praise for-ever."

In spite of his globe and its pompous inscription, Bartholomew gained nothing from the Court of England but vague promises. Although another Genoese, John Cabot, was given a fleet by the merchants of Bristol to search for the Island of Brazil, Bartholomew was forced to set out in 1491 for France, where he presented his petitions to a lady whom he vaguely calls "Madame de Bourbon"—apparently either Anne de Beaujeu, or her sister, the wife of the Admiral de Bourbon.

In these matters, Christopher and Bartholomew were acting as partners. But in those days of undeveloped communication, it was not always possible for the one to keep informed of the activities of the other. In fact, during the period of Christopher's difficulties, it would seem that the two brothers lost all touch with each other for a long time.

So now Christopher, in his turn, decided to make overtures to the Court of France. While awaiting the reply—and no doubt because he had no other means of subsistence—he left Cordova and sought the hospitality of the Duke of Medina-Cœli, at Seville. The Duke, full of interest in his project, immediately promised to maintain him while he stayed in Spain, and began the first moves to reinstate him in the Queen's favor. While this went on, Columbus returned to the convent of La Rabida where, beside the encouragement of his friends, Father Juan Perez and Antonio de Marchena, he found much to strengthen his convictions in talks with the mariners in the harbor below.

This port of Palos, in those days, was of considerable importance. It was one of the terminals for trade with the Canaries, the Azores and Guinea, and a port of contraband for the commerce which the Spaniards attempted with those African tribes on whom Portugal was supposed to hold the monopoly. It was a center for slave-traders, too, for Palos had a royal privilege on that commerce which it exercised indiscriminately on Negroes and on Arabs—were not all the infidel equal before the Lord?

Here Christopher made the acquaintance of the pilot Pedro Vasquez de la Frontera. The old seaman, who had accompanied the Infante of Portugal on many of his journeys, was firmly convinced that land could be found beyond the western oceans. Another pilot, from the port of Santa Maria, near Cadiz, swore that he had seen with his own eyes that distant shore. And among these simple mariners, Columbus met another, of greater importance but equally filled with the passion for discovery, who brought further confirmation of the Idea which had occupied Christopher for more than ten years.

Every provincial town has its one great local family, of

unmeasured respect and unquestioned authority within the small domain. In the case of Palos, this was the Pinzon family, hereditary shipbuilders, ship-owners and ship-captains to the town's fleets. The then head of the family, Martin-Alonso Pinzon, enjoyed a comfortable fortune, a lively ambition, and no excess of scruples. He had sailed far, on one occasion visiting Rome, with a cargo of sardines. While there, the dream of more profitable freight took hold of him, and he visited the Pontifical Library, to confer with a "counsellor of Pope Innocent III", engaged there.

The scholar showed him a map portraying the "Indian Islands of the Ocean Sea". This map was probably one of those engraved by Gratiosus Benincasa, who enjoyed a great reputation at that time. Benincasa was not lacking in imagination; he was more prone to mix conjecture with fact than even his most speculative contemporaries. Thus, on a chart which he made at Ancona in 1482 for a cardinal, he was not content merely to decorate the African coast with two large but hypothetical islands called Antilia and Salvago respectively—he showed their prospective discoverers in the act of finding them. Their fleet comprises a full-oared galleon and a smaller sailing ship, with a cross emblazoned on the canvas. One can see the rowers leaning to the oars in the final effort, while the captain, with his baton, points toward the new-found shore.

Pinzon the ambitious pored long over this attractive scene, picturing himself in the place of Benincasa's anonymous captain as his fleet approached the richer shore of the Indies. Such a voyage would be worth a thousand trips as a sardine freighter.

And the Counsellor of the Pope did not limit himself to maps and documents. He quoted directions attributed to Solomon: "Sail through the Mediterranean Sea to the point of Spain, heading thence toward the setting sun and holding neither to North nor to South; the way will be marked by temperate breezes and at the end you will come upon the land of Cipangu, which is so fertile and abundant in all things that with the riches thus gained you will be able to subjugate all Africa and Europe."

Thus Pinzon, too, had found his Toscanelli. A learned priest, full of disinterested benevolence, had shown him the Pope's own map, and taught him the wisdom of Solomon! He came back to Palos afire with eagerness for the enterprise.

The wanderer from Genoa encountered the small-town potentate; each learned enough of the other's plans to perceive their similarity. But a true union was impossible. The wealthy Pinzon, accustomed to rule his neighbors, and seeing the total poverty of his rival, would enter no partnership unless he himself could head it. Columbus, at best, might hope for the second place. But this foreigner with the strange power of will was not content with that. There was an exchange of courtesies, a mutual offer of aid and support—which must have seemed odd indeed on the part of the one—but at the end, the penniless visitor remained, invulnerable and inviolable, faithful to his dreams.

He was soon to give a still more striking proof of his firmness of resolve.

The aid of the Duke Medina-Cœli and of Juan Perez, as well as the fear that the King of France might profit by her indifference, had brought the Queen to a more favorable disposition toward Columbus. She sent for Perez.

The good friar was not rich enough to own a horse. To make the journey he rented a mule from a farmer, one Juan Rodriguez Cabezudo, and borrowed some money from the local magnate to pay the way. And thus, at midnight, he spread the skirts of his frock across the animal's back, raised the hood of his cape about his ears and set forth, the advance-courier of a journey that was to change the face of the world.

At the moment, the Kings were besieging Granada. While waiting the final reduction of this stronghold, which had annoyed them "like a pebble in the shoe," they had caused to be constructed outside the walls a sumptuous tented city, called the Camp of Santa-Fe—the Camp of Holy Faith. Here they heard Perez. Hither, soon, Columbus

100

was commanded. He came, pleaded his cause, and presented the sovereigns with a mariner's chart.

M. Charles de La Roncière has recently published a chart found in the Bibliothèque Nationale which has every appearance of being the one in question. The lettering of its legends, done with great care, shows that the map was destined for some important personage. Its date can be fixed as between 1488 and 1493. Its text is almost identical with that found among the marginalia noted by Columbus in his copy of the *Imago Mundi*.

The designer of the map, obviously a Genoese, indicates cities by their churches, and the countries—particularly those in Africa—by the products they export, such as ostrich plumes, pepper, cotton, or sugar cane. Genoa, among the cities, is drawn with especial care. And one of the African archipelagos is marked by the explanatory note: "These Isles are called in Italian, *Cavo Verde*; in Latin, *Promontorium Viride*. They were discovered by a Genoese named Antonio de Noli, from whom they took their name, which they still retain. Wheat grows there, but never comes to maturity because of the swarms of grasshoppers which devour it while still green. The best sugar cane and cotton are found here in abundance, as well as all sorts of fruit, which can be picked at all seasons of the year."

Now, Columbus, from his training as supercargo with

101

the fleets of the Centurione and the di Negri, had reason to feel a special interest in the wheat and sugar cane which had been their chief articles of importation.

Out in the western ocean, the map is embellished with islands imagined to be found there. "Here," says the legend, "lies the Island of the Seven Cities, already inhabited by Portugese colonists, according to the Spanish cadets; it is said that the sands of this island are rich in silver."

Near where Newfoundland should lie, Brazil is indicated. And in western Asia, the location of Cathay is marked with the legend: *Hic moratur*—Here He lives.

The mysterious He is none other than the Grand Khan, ruler of the Indies and its treasures,—so omnipresent in the minds of all that it is unnecessary to particularize his name.

Again, a legend that makes Columbus' authorship almost indisputable: *"De mari rubro longitudo ejus est sex mensium navigationis ut Hieronymus dicit in epistola ad Eliacum Monacum et de ibi annum integrum usque ad Indiam unde refert quod classis Salomonis per triennium ab India deportabat commercia."*

This, in its entirety, even to the solecism, *de ibi,* is almost identical with the quoted note from Pierre d'Ailly in Christopher's *Imago Mundi.* Again, in the same volume, a note in the margin says: *Et vide in nostris cartis a papiri ubi est spera.*—"See also our charts drawn on paper, where will be found a sphere"—and the map found by M. de la Roncière is drawn on paper, and has subjoined a representation of a sphere, containing the known world.

In any event, whether the map be actually one of Columbus' making, it is certainly of a type similar to the one with which he paid his homage to the Kings. He could not know what dangerous results his gift was to have.

His propositions, and the map with them, were submitted to another royal commission. The learned members heard all whose opinions might have weight—cosmographers, scholars, sailors, and theologians. Among all but the last, the testimony seemed to favor Columbus. But the map had thrown the theologians into an uproar. It was an embodiment of heresy. Here was the whole southern continent indicated to be populated, and had not Nicholas de Lyre expressly stated that no one lived below the line of the known world? Had not Saint Augustine declared that the antipodes were barren and deserted?

Columbus, suddenly, found himself menaced with an examination by the Tribunal of the Inquisition—in those days no light danger. Geraldini, who had been a member of the conference, saved the situation. He hurried to the Cardinal Mendoza, offering against the sophistries of the churchmen the proof of the Portuguese discoveries, furnishing incontestable evidence that the theologians could not forecast the world's surface from their texts. He argued that if the Portuguese found men living where the churchly theorists had said they could not be, Columbus might do as much again. The heresy, if any, would be on the part of the churchmen. The Cardinal was impressed by the logic of the subtle Florentine, and Christopher escaped the Question.

And now Granada had fallen; the *Reconquista* had come to a glorious conclusion. Flushed with victory, the happy Queen turned a welcoming ear to the Genoese who had waited so long and so patiently for the Court's favor. Another commission was formed, who, says Las Casas, "interviewed many sailors and sea-captains." Most important of all, "the question of expenses, and the rewards Columbus might demand, were all discussed." It seemed the end was in sight.

For seven years now, Christopher had lived from hand to mouth, depending on his friends' bounty, and what little he could pick up in the irregular occupations that presented themselves. It was not expected that he would boggle at the price now, when at last his dream seemed near to realization. But there was a strain of obstinacy in the man; he would hold to what he considered just, though it meant his ruin. And here, at the Camp of Santa-Fe, he made the same conditions he had demanded, and been refused, in Portugal.

He must be knighted; he must be given the prerogatives of a First Admiral; he must be accorded the hereditary vice-regency of all the lands, islands or continents he discovered; he must receive the tenth part of all revenues and profits obtained from them.

It was obvious that, if his expedition succeeded, Columbus by these terms would become overnight one of the most powerful personages of the realm. The commission was outraged.

Faced with their indignation, Columbus did not waver. He refused to reduce his demands in any way. The commission declined to accept them.

Once more, Columbus left the Presence—this time, it seemed, forever. The two Kings, with a polished irony, wished him God-speed on his way.

By how fine a thread, sometimes, is man's destiny divided! How easily could it have happened that Columbus had stamped his way out across the frontier and dragged wearily up the dusty roads of France to Paris, and to the Court of Charles VIII, the young King, careless even in his ambitions, of whom Comines wrote the epitome when he said, "He was little learned, but so good that it was impossible to find a better creature."

There the weary round of solicitations would have begun once more, while the King galloped after his armies from

Florence to Flanders and back again. And at last the suit is won, the expedition on its way. He returns; for a few years France, instead of Spain, enjoys the profit of the discovery. He receives, like his pretended cousin, Bissipat-Columbus, the grant of domains in Normandy and there, in his *chateau-fort*, his name transformed to "Messire Christofle Coulon," perhaps, he ends his days in peace and meditation.

Or another, and more probable outcome, might be imagined, in which Columbus, worn by the delays of the Spanish Court, might have been completely broken by the rebuffs of the French. His dream—as is the way with dreams—growing more vivid in his own eyes as the possibility of its realization faded, he might have grown gray and died there, supported by the alms doled out to him by his compatriots in the *rue des Lombards*, flouted by the palace guards and tolerated, among the other hangers-on, by the gentry for the laughter his rags and his pretensions might provoke.

His destiny, however, was to be saved, for his own and the Spanish glory, by the vision and persistence of a Jewish financier. Luis de Santangel held the office of *Escribano de racion*—Comptroler and Chancelor to the Court of Aragon. One of the wealthiest families in Spain, the de Santangel were *marranos*—converted Jews—and were known as the fiercest opponents of the Inquisition. The plotting which, in

1485, resulted in the assassination of the Grand Inquisitor Pedro Arbues was traced to the doors of their mansion in Saragossa. Naturally, in the years that followed, the Holy Office bent every effort to achieve their downfall; in the persecution that followed even the dead were not spared, and the bodies of the de Santangels long dead were exhumed and their bones degraded. Luis de Santangel owed his escape to the friendship of Ferdinand.

He was a man of many parts, not the least important, in those days, being the gift of making himself indispensable to his sovereign. A curious testimony, both to his importance and to the strange mixture of mysticism and the didactic that was the religion of the period, is in the fact he was eventually granted letters-patent by the King, guaranteeing him against all imputation of heresy!

Luis de Santangel was also a power in foreign commerce. The fact of his birth, too, kept him in touch with the other great Jewish traders. To such a man, the pretensions of Christopher did not seem so fantastic as to others; within his own experience, he had the means to judge their practicability. And so, at the crisis in Columbus' fortunes, he appeared to plead for him.

The risk, he argued, was not great. Columbus asked only for a few ships, and the money to outfit them. If the expedition failed, this would be the only loss. And if it succeeded, what a magnificent profit the Crown would reap! The chances of failure, he admitted, were ten times greater than the single chance of success—but the rewards of success would be a thousand, or a million times the cost. The prize, he reminded them, was the wealth of Cathay. If they, for the price of a few ships, refused to reach for it, it might well fall to the French King's grasp. Meanwhile, Columbus was hurrying on toward Paris.

Courtiers are like sheep. When one has the courage to lead the way, there are always others who will follow. So now, at the example of Luis de Santangel, a dozen others—Juan Cabrero, Chamberlain to the King; the Dominican friar, Diego de Deza, tutor to the Prince; Donna Juana Velasquez, his nurse; Gabriel Sanchez, Treasurer of Aragon; Alexander Geraldini and many others of the Court—came to urge the support of Columbus. And while these mighty personages were pleading his cause in the council chamber, his old friends the Franciscan friars were working in their quieter, deeper ways to bring about his recall.

And now, to the solicitations of a Jew and a monkish order, were added those of a woman.

This was the Donna Beatriz de Bobadilla, wife of Andres de Cabrera and favorite of the Queen since the very beginning of her reign. Neither the passage of years, nor the changes of fortune, or of morals, had weakened their intimacy. Cabrera—"our good servant"—became Marquis

de Moya; Beatriz became the mistress of Cardinal Mendoza. Isabella, so chaste herself, could condone the faults
of others. Her old friend was still "my daughter, the Mar-
quise." And now she too, for reasons which we can only
conjecture at this day, became an enthusiastic advocate of
Columbus' plans.

No record remains of the pleading and cajolery they
used to sway the Kings. No one knows what argument
it was that finally brought them to their decision.

All that even Columbus knew was that two leagues out
on the road from Granada, as its walls and towers were
fading into the distance, an alguazil, riding hard, over-
took him. The Queen had ordered his recall.

Three months later, on April 17, 1492, the two Kings
put their signatures to a contract drawn between them and
Columbus, by the Royal Secretary of Aragon.

The conditions asked, and which Your Majesties
give and accord to Don Christopher Columbus in such
sort as to repay him for what he may discover in
the Ocean Sea, and for the voyage which, with the
aid of God, he is now undertaking in the service of
Your Majesties, are as follows:

Firstly, that Your Majesties, by virtue of Your dominion over the said Ocean Sea, do create the said
Don Christopher Your Admiral in all islands and

continents which by his effort and industry may be discovered and acquired in the said Ocean Sea, through the extent of his life, and, after his death, his heirs and successors one after the other perpetually, with all the preëminences and prerogatives pertaining to the said rank, and such as Don Alonso Enrriques, Your Grand Admiral of Castille, and the other predecessors in the said rank, enjoyed and possessed in their domains.

Agreed by Their Majesties,

(*Signed*) JUAN DE COLOMA.

Similarly, that Your Majesties ordain the said Don Christopher Your Vice-Regent and Governor-General over all the said islands and continents and islands which he may discover and acquire in the said Seas; and that, for the governing of all and each of the these islands, he shall himself choose three persons for each office, and that of these Your Majesties shall choose and designate the one most pleasing to You, in order that in this way the lands which we may by the Grace of the Almighty be permitted to discover and acquire to the service of Your Majesties will best be governed.

Agreed by Their Majesties,

(*Signed*) JUAN DE COLOMA.

110

Item, that of all and every kind of merchandise, whether pearls, precious stones, gold, silver, spices and all other kinds of products and merchandise of whatever name and kind may be, which are found, or bartered, or bought or taken within the limits of the said Admiralty, that of these Your Majesties do from henceforth grant to the said Don Christopher and ordain that he shall take and have for himself the tenth part after deduction shall have been made for expenditures which shall have been made, to the end that he shall take and have for himself the tenth part of the entire profits and shall so take at his pleasure, leaving the other nine parts to the profit of Your Majesties.

Agreed by Their Majesties,
(*Signed*) JUAN DE COLOMA.

Similarly, that if by reason of the merchandise which he may bring back from the said islands or continents which may, as has been specified, be acquired or discovered, or from such merchandise as may be acquired here from other merchants in exchange for that brought from the said islands and continents, there may arise some suit or civil process in the place and location where the said commerce and traffic shall have occurred, and if, by reason of

111

the preëminence of his rank of admiral, it shall be his duty to take cognizance of the said suit, then shall it be agreed by Your Majesties that he or his lieutenant, and no other judge, shall decide the suit, at no matter what time it may be brought.

> Agreed by Their Majesties, if such suit be within the jurisdiction of the Admiral, and under similar jurisdiction to that held by the Admiral Don Alonso Enrriques, and his predecessors in their domain, and if the cause be just,
>
> (*Signed*) JUAN DE COLOMA.

Item, that, in all the ships which may be commissioned for the said commerce and traffic, on each occasion when they may be so commissioned, the said Don Christopher Columbus, if he desire, may contribute and pay the eighth part of that which may be spent in the enterprise, and that then he may take and have for himself the eighth share of the profits which may be made.

> Agreed by Their Majesties,
>
> (*Signed*) JUAN DE COLOMA.

Granted and accorded with the agreement of Your Majesties at the end of each item. In the city of Santa-

Fe de la Vega de Granada, the seventeenth day of April in the year of our Lord Jesus Christ, 1492.

I, THE KING.   I, THE QUEEN.

By command of the King and of the Queen, *Registered, Talcena.*   JUAN DE COLOMA.

Subsequent letters-patent, dated April 20, 1492, make the Vice-Regency a hereditary appurtenance to Columbus: "Your son and successors, in the said rank and functions, shall call themselves and be entitled Don, Admiral, Vice-Regent and Governor."

This was the famous "Capitulation," a treaty between the Most Catholic Kings and the son of the Genoese weaver,—in its terms, in the wealth it aspired to apportion, a document more fantastic than the wildest conceptions of romance. It was obvious, however, that the rewards it promised were contingent on the fulfilment of its conditions. Columbus must first find his Vice-Regency and Admiralty in the Ocean Sea, before he could rule over them.

The immediate question was one of money. Santangel advanced him 1,140,000 maravedis. Ferdinand refused to gamble on so risky an enterprise. The money which his Chancellor paid from the treasury of Aragon was therefor credited against that of Castille.

There were other contributors whose names now are unknown. Columbus himself ·undertook one-eighth of the

113

costs, and the fact that he obtained the money is a tribute to his skill in the art of borrowing. Here, perhaps, the training his lean years had given stood him in good stead now, when he could offer half a world for security.

Juanoto Berardi, a Florentine ship-builder established at Seville, lent him 180,000 maravedis. His compatriots, Jacopo di Negro, Luis Doria, and a certain Catapal, furnished him the rest. Curiously, the name of the Centurione does not appear in the list of those who financed his enterprise; their branch at Granada could hardly have been in ignorance of the expedition.

Meanwhile, the Chancellor was preparing a passport, in which the Kings recommended to all the soverigns he might encounter, their servant "the noble gentleman Christopher Columbus, who is charged with certain duties and enterprises affecting the service of God and the increase of the Christian faith, as well as Our advantage and profit."

But so general a greeting did not suffice for the explorer's purpose. "Since it was his firm belief," says Las Casas, "that not only would he discover these islands and continents, but that also he would reach to the realm of the Grand Khan and the rich lands of Cathay, as he had been advised by the Doctor, Paul (Toscanelli) he asked that the Kings give him letters of introduction to the Grand Khan, and to the Kings and Princes of the Indies, and to

114

all other kingdoms he might enter, in the lands he expected to discover."

To his other credentials, then, was added a letter to the Grand Khan and the other Tartaric princes, assuring them of the good health and happy state of the Kings, and informing them of Their good will.

At the moment, the town of Palos, as a result of certain misdeeds, had been condemned to furnish the Crown with two caravels and to maintain their costs for twelve months in the royal service. These ships were now, by the Crown's decree, turned over to Christopher. Another decree declared that all judgments, civil or criminal, would be waived for any person undertaking the journey under the noble captain Christopher Columbus.

On the twenty-third of May, 1492, the royal pronouncement was read by a notary in the church of Saint George of Palos, enjoining the townspeople to furnish within ten days two caravels, completely equipped, to Christopher Columbus, sent "as Our appointed captain . . . into certain parts of the Ocean Sea, on matters of Our service."

Christopher might well congratulate himself that the end of his troubles was at hand. And yet he was to encounter another obstacle in the sullen, clannish spirit of a provincial town, and its hatred of the foreigner. He had authority from the Queen—but the Queen was far away.

Martin-Alonzo Pinzon, the autocrat of Palos, regarded his former rival with mixed emotions, where a patrician disdain for the poor adventurer blent with the awe of the provincial at a man who had breathed the air of the Court. Columbus, from the very start, had shown no disposition to propitiate the other. And now Pinzon had his revenge in secretly fomenting a passive rebellion against the royal decrees.

On June 20 Juan de Peñasola, member of the Queen's bodyguard, appeared at Palos, and seized a caravel, the *Pinta*, in the name of the Crown. Several other ships were requisitioned from Andalusia. But still the general apathy prevailed. And what hope of success could there be in such a venture, with a reluctant crew that grudged the very ships they sailed in? It seemed that the good will of Pinzon must, after all, be obtained.

Columbus, therefor, began to treat with the stubborn Martin-Alonzo. He could not, naturally, show him the letters and maps he had obtained from Toscanelli; the Genoese had learned his lesson in a hard school. Moreover, to admit that his plan had been submitted to the Portuguese, and had been refused by these dare-devils of the seas, was hardly a method calculated to convince Pinzon or anyone else of its chances for success. Columbus, therefor, recopied Toscanelli's letter, omitting all mention of the Portuguese, and replacing the name of Toscanelli by such locutions as, "several men of great learning," or "several other merchants of wide experience." [1]

It was necessary, however, not merely to flatter Pinzon, but to excite his interest in more practical fashion, by offering him a share in the profits of the expedition. In Spain, as the "Capitulation" of the Kings well reveals, it was the custom to solemnize such agreements by lengthy, meticulously-worded contracts. The absence of any such record of the treaty between Christopher and Pinzon is, therefore, all the more remarkable. It may be, of course, that the veteran sardine trader, dazzled by the legend of Cathay, considered any stipulations superfluous concerning a treasure so great that even its ten-thousandth part would equal a king's ransom. Or perhaps, and more shrewdly still, he was persuaded that so consummate a mariner and merchant as himself could, the better for the absense of all treaty, assume complete charge of the undertaking, once the fleet was at sea.

In any case, Pinzon intervened, rallying sailors and ship owners to his authority. Vessels that had suddenly disappeared from the harbor as suddenly reappeared again. With the *Pinta*, Columbus chose two others among these:

[1] This letter, found among Columbus' papers after his death, was first published as a second letter from Toscanelli. It remained for M. N. Lumien, in his study of Toscanelli, to make it clear that it was in reality the first letter, altered in Columbus' copy, as explained above.

117

THE EMBARCATION AT PALOS
AUGUST 2, 1492.

" 'Having perfected all his preparations, Thursday, August 2, 1492, Christopher Columbus ordered all his people to embark, and the next day, Friday, which was the third of the same month of August, half an hour before sunrise, he ordered the sails raised and went out of the harbor and bar which is called Saltes, because the river of Palos is so named'."

—From the *Journal* of Columbus.

118

the *Gallega*, whose name he changed to the *Santa-Maria*, and a tiny sloop, the *Nina*. The *Santa-Maria*, described by Peter Martyr d'Anghiera as "a cargo vessel, decked over," had a length over all of about 125 feet—about the size of a Banks fisherman today. The two others were barely half as large. All, however, were decked; the *Santa-Maria* had a wooden housing over the poop-deck, and a smaller deck-house forward. She mounted three masts, square-rigged. The *Pinta* carried similar deck-housing, and the same rig. The *Nina*, however, had only the after-deck housed, and carried the lateen rig still seen occasionally in the Mediterranean.

The artillery they mounted consisted of bombards and espingardes, a sort of wide-mouthed, short-barreled mortar, throwing balls of stone, or of lead hooped with iron. All three flew the royal pennon: a green cross with the insignia *F* and *Y*; the sails, too, were decorated with a crqss. The *Santa-Maria* also flew its own standard, showing a Christ, crucified, on a black ground.

While the little fleet was being made ready, Pinzon began to organize the crews. Among these he included five of his family—his sons, his brothers and a nephew. The rest he drummed up in the inns of Palos. "Come, towns-men!" he would argue. "Sign with us for this voyage. We go where even the lowliest houses are roofed with tiles of thick gold! Come with us, friends; if you do you'll come home again richer in wealth than any prince." With such inducements, there were few who refused. Sailors, quartermasters, boatswains to double the number needed, soon were begging for berths on the caravals.

Columbus chose under him, as fleet-commander, a Genoese mariner. The Captain of the *Santa-Maria* remained: Juan de La Cosa, skilled pilot and cosmographer, a native of Santona. Messer Alonzo de Maguer was the ship's doctor, and Diego de Arana, a nephew of Beatriz de Bobadilla, was the *alguazil-major*, or chief disciplinary officer. Martin-Alonzo Pinzon himself commanded the *Pinta*, and carried his brother, Francisco-Martin, as chief quartermaster. The younger brother, Vincente-Yanez, commanded the *Nina*, having for quartermaster Pero Alonzo Nino.

The matter of conversing with the Grand Khan, once he had been met with, was not overlooked. The choice of an interpreter was the more difficult for that no one, naturally, knew what language the legendary potentate might speak. Eventually Luis de Torre, a converted Jew, with a knowledge of Hebrew, Chaldean and Arabic, was designated for the important post. The crew was made up of about eighty Biscayan mariners, reinforced by twenty-four convicts, released, by virtue of their enlistment, from the prisons of Palos and Huelva.

The Crown was represented by a committee of four, to protect its interests and report on the findings of the expedition. These were: Rodrigo Sanchez de Segovia, artillery officer; Pedro Guttierez, an officer of the Treasury; the goldsmith, Castillo, metallurgist and expert in the only metal they expected to discover; and Rodrigo de Escovedo, notary to the King.

The whole complement numbered one hundred and twenty. A minute inquiry into the salaries and general expenses of the expedition has been made by Mr. John Boyd Thacher. According to his conclusions, the salaries for the eight months' service totaled 268,000 maravedis; the sum of all expenditures was 1,167,542 maravedis, or, reduced to the coinage of today, $7,203.

Of this, the Crown furnished one million maravedis—a little more than $6,000. For this investment, the lands of Columbus' discovery were to return them, during the succeeding century, an amount of gold alone to the value of $1,750,000!

And now at last, the preparations were complete. Furbished and garlanded, the three little caravels lay in the harbor of Palos, ready aweigh for the starting. For a hundred years, their destination had been the focus of men's eyes, and in that time many minds had meditated a similar excursion. We have long been accustomed to believe that Columbus was the first to conceive the earth as round, the first to propound the paradox of sailing west to reach the east. Neither the one nor the other assertion is true. Columbus began with theories that many men had considered, but he compounded them, synthesized them, narrowed and compacted them to the point and purpose of his will, and proved them practical. His honor lies in that, though he dreamed other men's dreams, he had the courage and the tenacity to distil their essence into reality.

The last day came. Fernando, Christopher's child by Beatriz Enriquez, until now the charge of the monks at La Rabida, was sent back to its young mother at Cordova by the same mule which the friar, Juan Perez, had borrowed from Cabesudo for his midnight voyage to the Queen. At the last moment, too, the Court, until now indifferent, developed a sudden interest in the journey. Isabella promised a pension of 10,000 maravedis, drawn on the markets of Seville, to the sailor who should first sight the land they sought.

At dawn, on the third of August, 1492, the pennants broke to the breeze and the moorings were loosed. While the townspeople watched and cheered from the mole, the little flotilla moved slowly out into the harbor. Square-rig and lateen-rig, the fresh sails crawled up the masts and took the wind, and the ships' prows plunged to the swell of the ocean. The watchers saw the banners twinkle and fade, saw the sails gleam in the rising sun, and the masts sway. Then all merged in the blue of the horizon.

Aboard the three ships, under the green cross of the Crown and the black cross of Christ, the hundred and twenty voyagers—crafty Pinzon and deep-eyed Columbus, the King's commissioners, the swarthy mariners and the shaven convicts—embarked on the most daring voyage the world has ever known, were busied with the duties and preoccupations of the little sea-community that for eight months was to be their world.

V. THE VOYAGE OF DREAMS

THE voyage of Columbus has passed, for most of us, out of the realm of history and into the province of dreams. The ships he sailed in seem now, in our imaginations, scarcely larger than the toy-ships we ourselves launched in childhood, at the beach, and the whole aspect of his undertaking is tinged in our minds with the same romantic and impossible glamor of a child's adventuring.

We see the voyage in a series of tableaux, all as theatrical as the engravings which commemorate it. We see the Admiral, keen-eyed and vigilant, standing on the poop-deck of his flagship, staring out into the unknown. We see him, dauntless and inexorable, dominating the mutinous rabble of seamen, and pointing onward to the west. We see him, at last, on the shore of that island which he believed to be Cypangu, dropping dramatically on one knee to praise his deliverance, while the flag of Spain waves overhead, and naked, bewildered savages surround him.

Even as children, too, our knowledge today outstrips

124

his. Anybody could tell him now how to reach the Orient. There are weekly sailings from San Francisco, or you can go through the Canal if you have time. The latest news is that Lindbergh may fly there. And, as Columbus' aim was mistaken, his attainment becomes a little ludicrous, and so all the hopes that inspired him, the courage that prompted, the resolution that guided him become unreal, fantastic, in consequence.

His own Journal, when first read, does little to vivify the impression. A stern man, and reticent, Christopher was not likely to indulge in melodrama. Moreover, when the document was at last published, it had gone through a revision at the hands of the historian, Las Casas, and he had doubtless still further pruned it, eliminating all but the matter essential to the record of the journey.

And yet, when we read it again, the very leanness of it gives it eloquence, the very sparseness of it gives it poignance. Beneath the simple, matter-of-fact phrasing, we see, constantly moving, the tremendous uncertainty, the unending anxiety, the mounting torment with which its author's mind was filled as he wrote. Land, is its motive and its climax. At first expected, then longed for, at last almost despaired of, the fever for the sight of land dominates every page.

Read in that light, one begins to realize the triumph that was his, and the sincerity of emotion that brought him to his knees when, finally, he felt beneath his feet the sandy shore of the new world he had discovered.

The voyage begins uneventfully enough.[1]

Having perfected all his preparations, Thursday, August 2, 1492, Christopher Columbus ordered all his people to embark, and the next day, Friday, which was the third of the same month of August, half an hour before sunrise, he ordered the sails raised and went out of the harbor and bar which is called Saltes, because that river of Palos is so named.

> *Friday, August third:* We went with a strong sea breeze sixty miles, which are fifteen leagues, toward the south until sunset; afterwards to the south-west and to the south, one-quarter south-west, which was the way to the Canaries.
>
> *Saturday, August fourth:* We went to the south-west, one-quarter south.
>
> *Sunday, August fifth:* We went on our way, more than forty leagues between day and night . . .

And so onward, toward the Canaries. The friendly coast of the continent has long since disappeared. They are alone, but still not quite alone, for these are known waters. Other

[1] Excerpts quoted from the Journal are from *Christopher Columbus*, John Boyd Thatcher; Putnam, 1903, New York.

ships have come this way; they have not yet lost all touch with mankind.

Meanwhile, the little world that a ship at sea develops has been forming. Already a kind of rivalry is taking shape, between the impatient Martin-Alonzo, to whom the voyage is but a beginning, and the confident Columbus, to whom it is a long-awaited fulfillment. And there are other purposes at work.

On Monday, the sixth, the helm of the *Pinta* breaks, and the circumstances are such that the damage is suspected to have been not entirely accidental. Two of the mariners, Gomes Rascon and Cristobal Quintero, share owners in the vessel, are believed to be implicated. They have never been enthusiastic for the voyage, and the mishap was brought about perhaps in the hope that the *Pinta* would be sent back to Palos.

Soon after, the *Pinta* springs a leak. The little fleet limps on, arriving at Teneriffe Thursday, August ninth. Christopher had for a time intended to replace the *Pinta* with a more seaworthy craft, but they "repaired her very well," and she remained to share the honors of the voyage.

They lay there almost a month, refitting and revictualing, and during the stay saw "a great fire issue from the mountains of the island of Teneriffe, of which the greater part is very high." The apparition frightened many of the crew,

127

who took it for an ill omen, but Columbus had seen volcanoes before, and reassured them. Here, too, they saw "many honorable Spaniards," who "swore that each year they saw land to the west of the Canaries, and others from Gomera affirmed the same thing under oath."

Heartened by this testimony, then, they sailed on Thursday, September sixth, from the harbor of Gomera. They had need of haste. Columbus had learned that "three caravels from Portugal were sailing about there, in order to capture him: it must have been through the envy felt by the King of Portugal, because of the Admiral's going to Castille."

The enemy, however, were safely avoided. Columbus handed their sailing orders to each of his captains, commanding them to proceed with extreme caution, from midnight to dawn, once they had logged seven hundred leagues. The precaution was taken in order that they might not strike land unawares, in the night, and be wrecked. So, in the happiest ignorance of the enormous voyage that awaited them, they headed due west, into the unknown waters.

Sunday, September ninth: Went nineteen leagues and resolved to reckon less than he had gone, so that if the voyage should be a long one, his people would not be frightened and discouraged . . ."

The Admiral (who, throughout the Journal, is referred to in the third person) had learned to expect delays and a slow fulfillment. Land might be farther than they supposed, despite the evidence of the "honorable Spaniards."

> *Monday, September tenth:* . . . went sixty leagues at the rate of ten miles an hour, which are two and one-half leagues, but he computed only forty-eight leagues . . .
>
> *Wednesday, September twelfth:* This day, pursuing his course, they went thirty-three leagues during the night and day, computing less for the said reason . . .

And now they enter the zone of oceanic marvels:

> *Saturday, September fifteenth:* . . . sailed that day and night twenty-seven leagues upon his course to the west and somewhat more, and at the beginning of this night they saw a marvelous branch of fire fall from the heavens into the sea, four or five leagues distant from them . . .

Christopher, no doubt, had expected some such manifestation. Were not the unknown places on all the maps he had studied decorated by pictures of monsters and apparitions supposed to inhabit there? He had already informed his ship-mates that he had once seen a sea-serpent

DIANA LEADING COLUMBUS ON HIS WAY.

FROM A SEVENTEENTH CENTURY PRINT

"And now they enter the zone of oceanic marvels.
. . . The crew is again murmuring. . . . Suppose they
did find land, might it not be some unearthly, devilish
region, inhabited by those monsters they had heard
tell of . . . sea-serpents . . . sirens . . . ?"

or siren, on one of his voyages. Nevertheless, Las Casas says, quoting perhaps from one of the unpublished portions of the Journal, "All these things disturbed and saddened the sailors, and they commenced to think that they were signs they had not started on a good course."

One can picture the little group of mariners, so childlike amid the wonderment of the medieval universe, standing huddled in the well-deck amidships, staring up at the fiery writing in the sky, and then turning, with an awe for his learning that mingled distrust with reverence, to study the Admiral, pacing the poop above them.

But land still was believed to be not far distant. With the land of gold almost at their fingertips, they could afford to brave the elements, a little longer. And the elements continued kind.

Sunday, September 16: . . . Now and always from this time forward the air was extremely temperate, so that it was a great pleasure to enjoy the mornings and that nothing was lacking except to hear nightingales. . . . Here they began to see many tufts of very green grass, which according to appearance had not long been detached from the land, on which account everyone judged they were near some island: but not the continental land, according to the Admiral,

131

who says: "because I make the continental land farther onward". . . .

Monday, September 17: . . . the pilots took the position of the North Star, and they found that the needles declined to the north-west a good quarter, and the sailors were afraid and were troubled, and did not say for what reason. . . .

The most dangerous mutiny is mute. Though no one had spoken, Columbus understood. So, next morning at dawn, he took the position again—

showing the needles to be good, for the star varies and the needles do not. On this day, saw much more grass, and it was green from rivers, and found a live craw-fish which the Admiral kept. . . .

Moreover, the sea water was now found to be less salt than it had been observed before, since leaving the Canaries. The men all tasted of it, and affirmed this. Great schools of fish came from the west to play about the vessels. The breeze was soft and warm.

And suddenly one of those waves of pleasant apprehension that come over men strung with impatience, enveloped them—a mood more thrilling for its causelessness, the more trusted because unreasoning.

. . . They all became very joyful, and the fastest ships went onward, in order to be the first to land. . . .

The men sang and shouted to one another. The keenest-eyed among them were posted in the prow. But the day wore on, and no land appeared. The surge of anticipation died, rankling. They had at that time, Las Casas computes, made 370 leagues (about 1300 miles) from the Canaries. They were, in reality, little more than midway of the voyage.

Next day, however, some of yesterday's enthusiasm still remained.

Tuesday, September eighteenth: They made more than fifty-five leagues, but he counted only forty-eight. The sea was calm as in the River of Seville. This day Martin-Alonso with the Pinta, which was a fast sailer, did not wait for the others because he said to the Admiral from his caraval that he had seen a great number of birds go toward the west and that night he hoped to see land, and for that reason he was sailing so fast. . . . A large, dark cloud appeared in the north, which was a sign that land is near.

And still on—

Wednesday, September nineteenth: They made twenty-five leagues, but it was calm, and counted only twenty-two. This day, at ten o'clock, a pelican came to the ship, and another in the afternoon, these birds not accustomed to go more than twenty-leagues from land. . . . There were slight rains without wind, which is a certain indication of land. . . .

The one great preoccupation is worrying all their minds. Land . . . land . . . where is the land? The question lies in every sentence he writes. They have long since passed the spot where they conjectured it to lie. Where is the land?

Christopher refits his theory to the circumstance. On all his maps, the coast of Asia had been shown as protected by a vast archipelago of islands. He concludes that they must now be driving among those islands—

> . . . He was sure that to the north and toward the south there were some islands . . . and that he was going between them, because it was his desire to go forward toward the Indies while the weather is pleasant. On the return they should see all. . . .

They sail on, for the continent. More birds come to greet them, and a sailor catches one by hand, which was "like a river-bird, not a sea-bird, the feet being like those of a gull." At dawn, more birds come singing to the ship, remaining till sunset.

Friday, September twenty-first: Most of the day calm. . . . Toward midday they saw a whale, which is an indication that they were near land, because they always remain near it. Also much grass. . . .

The grass, first welcomed as a good omen, was becoming an annoyance. They were now traversing that eddy of the ocean currents called the Sargasso Sea, center of surface flotsam and driftwood; the farther they went, the thicker became the grass—

. . . "This grass sometimes cheered them," says Las Casas, "believing they would soon see land; sometimes made them despair, fearing to strike upon some rock in it, and sometimes those who were steering the ships turned in order not to enter it, because it was so thick that it appeared to retard the vessels."

Saturday, September twenty-second: . . . They sailed west, north-west, tacking from one point to the other, and made thirty leagues against the head wind. The Admiral says here: "This contrary wind was very necessary to me, because my people were becoming very much excited, as they thought that on these seas no winds blew in order to return to Spain." In the morning there was no weed, but in the afternoon it was very thick.

135

And onward still they sail. Doves are seen, and more of the strange river-birds, white in color. The sea is thick with grass, and the grass alive with crabs. The crew is again murmuring, "saying that in this ocean there was no sea and no wind that would ever bring them back to Spain." The old legends of men who had vanished over the earth's rim came back to torment them. Would they, too, share that unimaginable fate? The hour of terror had come; the men ranged the deck in groups; fear rose uncontrollably within them, like a tide.

Land had been promised them. The Admiral had promised that he would show them the Indies; he had promised them gold, and had marked for them on the chart where they should find it. But now every one knew they had long since sailed far beyond the distance he had estimated, and still no land was visible.

And if he had erred in this, why not in his other conjectures? Suppose they did find land, might it not prove to be, not the Indies, but some unearthly, devilish region, inhabited by those monsters they had heard tell of—brutes with the bodies of men and the faces of dogs, savages whose heads grew in their stomachs, women with hawk-talons, many-headed giants whose glance petrified?

The men muttered and grumbled among themselves, and Columbus watched them. No tangible authority remained to him now. The King, the Queen, the letters-patent they had given him, his certificate of command—all these had lost their power when the ship's prow first turned into unfamiliar waters. The men grumbled, and moved sullenly when ordered. And he could not press his orders, for fear of open rebellion. But though he might not domineer, he still could dominate. His will drove them on. . . .

"My friend," counselled Martin-Alonso, "why don't you hang half a dozen of these grumblers? Or if you don't want to be bothered, say the word and I'll handle the matter myself."

Christopher knew better than to adopt such summary measures. The foreigner must always speak more softly than the native. Though the Queen had made him her Admiral, he was still, to these provincials, an outlander. He moved among them, persuading, cajoling, taking care to point out every omen that seemed favorable.

Sunday, September twenty-third: He sailed to the north-west and at times to the north quarter and at times on his course, which was to the west, and they went as much as 22 leagues. . . . They saw a turtle dove and a pelican, and another small river bird . . . and as the sea was calm and quiet the people murmured, saying that, since there was not much sea in that region, the wind would never blow for the return to Spain: but afterwards the sea rose greatly and without wind, which terrified them, and because of which the Admiral says here: "So that the high sea was very necessary to me, as it came to pass once before in the time when the Jews went out of Egypt with Moses, who took them from Captivity."

Monday, September twenty-fourth: . . . Sailed on the west course all day and all night, making fourteen leagues . . . Counted only twelve. . . .

The most terrible quality of ignorance is its stubbornness. Minds to which ideas come slowly are equally slow in changing them. Reason can not refute them. Words dazzle them. They listen to your arguments, turn away silently, as if convinced; you are overjoyed—until, a moment later, they are back again, perverse and unheeding, their convictions as strong as ever.

This was the state of mind Columbus had to struggle against. Of active insurrection there was none—unless Oviedo's unsupported story is to be believed, the mutiny legend falls to the ground. But, for days and days, Christopher faced a more sullen menace—the *threat* of mutiny. Without doubt there were times when he would almost have welcomed an active rebellion, to clear the air.

Meanwhile, all he knew was that the men looked sullenly, gathered in groups, spoke together in undertones, and ceased when he approached. He still sailed westward.

The men thought it was madness to go farther. Was it not enough glory for them, that they had sailed deeper into the west than any one ever had gone before? What of the return? Even now, if they turned back at once, there would be hardly enough food left to bring them home again. "Some went further," Las Casas writes, "saying that if he persisted in going onward, that the best thing of all was to throw him in the sea some night, publishing that he had fallen while taking the position of the star with his quadrant or astrolabe, and that as he was a foreigner, little or no account would be taken of the matter . . . and as the other sailors were natives and citizens of Palos and Moguel, they all went to them (the Pinzons) and made cause with them: of these Pinzons, Christopher Columbus complained greatly and of the trouble they had given him."

Tuesday, September twenty-fifth: The Admiral talked with Martin-Alonso, Captain of the other caravel, the Pinta, in regard to a chart which he had sent to Martin-Alonso three days before, on which, as it appears, the Admiral had drawn certain islands, in that sea, and Martin-Alonzo said they were in that region, and the Admiral replied that it appeared so to him: but since they had not encountered them, it must have been caused by the currents which had continually forced the ships to the north-east, and because they had not gone as far as the pilots said: and then having arrived at this conclusion the Admiral directed Martin-Alonso to send him the said chart and it being sent by a cord the Admiral began to mark out places upon it with his pilot and sailors. At sunset Martin-Alonso mounted in the stern of his ship and with great joy called to the Admiral, begging a reward from him as he saw land: and when the Admiral heard him affirm this, he says that he commenced on his knees to give thanks to Our Lord, and Martin-Alonso said *Gloria in Excelsis Deo* with his people: the Admiral's people did the same and the people on the Nina all ascended the mast and the rigging: and all affirmed that it was land, and it appeared so to the Admiral and that it might be 25 leagues away. They all affirmed until night that it was land. . . .

It was, however, another mirage of the imagination. They sailed on.

Wednesday, September twenty-sixth: They went thirty-two leagues during day and night, and he computed for the people twenty-four. The sea was like a river, the breezes pleasant and mild.

140

So they bore on their way, seeing many *"dorados"*—giltheads—and killing one, the weather continuing kind and the sea gentle, so that many of the sailors dropped overside, for a swim in the warm waters. . . .

Tuesday, October second: He sailed on his way to the west, 39 leagues day and night: the sea continually calm and favorable. *Many thanks be given God,* said the Admiral here. Grass came, from the east to the west, contrary to what had happened before. . . .

And again, next day, the tide of rebellion rose again, "As he did not wish to beat about on all sides in search of the islands which the pilots believed lay near there, more especially Martin-Alonso, they all commenced to mutiny, and the disagreement would have gone further if God had not put out his hand as usual, showing them immediately new signs of being near land." Petrels appeared, flying about the ships' masts, and " a great quantity of grass, some very old and some very fresh, and it bore a kind of fruit". . . .

Thursday, October fourth: He sailed on his way. . . .

Friday, October fifth: Sailed on his course, going about eleven miles an hour . . . the sea pleasant and calm. . . .

Two days later, their hopes were raised and dashed again.

> *Sunday, October seventh:* This day the caravel Nina, which was ahead on account of being a fast sailer, raised a banner on top of the mast and fired a lombard, as a signal that they saw land. . . .

But the echo of the cannon died again, and the silence of the barren waters remained. Had they, men asked themselves, sailed utterly beyond the world's limits? Was there no land anywhere?

> . . . He ordered that the vessels should all unite at sunrise and sunset, because these two times are most suitable for seeing a long distance. . . .
>
> *Monday, October eighth:* . . . Saw jays, ducks and a pelican. . . .
>
> *Tuesday, October ninth:* Sailed to the south-west and went 5 leagues.. . . All night they heard birds passing . . .
>
> *Wednesday, October tenth:* Here the people could no longer suffer the journey. They complained at the long voyage: but the Admiral encouraged them as well as he was able, giving them good hope of the benefits they would receive, and adding that for the rest it was useless to complain, since he had come in

search of the Indies and thus he must pursue his journey until he found them, with the aid of the Lord. . . .

And old Martin-Alonso, for once agreeing, swore that he "would sail a year, if need be, till he reached the Indies!"

Thursday, October eleventh: He sailed to the west south-west. They had a much higher sea than they had had in all the voyage. They saw petrels, and a green branch near the ship . . . and a little branch of dog-roses. With these signs every one breathed and rejoiced. . . .

After sunset, he sailed on his first course, to the west. They went about twelve miles each hour and up to two hours after midnight they went about 90 miles, which are 20½ leagues. And because the caravel Pinta was the best sailor and was going ahead of the Admiral, land was discovered by her people and the signs which the Admiral had ordered were made. A sailor called Rodrigo de Traina saw this land first, although the Admiral at ten o'clock at night, being in the stern forecastle, saw a light, but it was so concealed that he would not declare it to be land: but he called Pedro Guttierez, Groom of the Chamber of the King, and said to him that it appeared to be a

143

light and asked him to look at it: he did, and saw it. He also told Rodrigo Sanchez de Segovia, whom the King and Queen sent with the fleet as Inspector, who saw nothing because he was not where he could see it. After the Admiral told it, it was seen once or twice, and it was like a small wax candle, which rose and fell,[2] which hardly appeared to be an indication of land. But the Admiral was certain that they were near land. For this reason, when they said the *Salve*, which all the sailors are in the habit of saying and singing in their way, and they were all assembled together, the Admiral implored and admonished them to guard the stern forecastle well and search diligently for land, and said that to whomever should first see land he would then give a silk doublet, beside the other gifts which the Kings had promised them, to whomever should first see land. At two hours after midnight the land appeared, from which they were about two leagues distant.. They lowered all the sails and remained with the cross-jack-sail, which is the great sail without bonnets, and lay-to, standing off and on, until the day, Friday.

That day, October twelfth, 1492, and early in the morn-

[2] Fernando Columbus supposed this light to have been that of a torch carried by one of the native Indians, "who had the custom of carrying a piece of fire-brand, when they went out from their huts at night."

ing, they dropped anchor before the land and went ashore. A new hemisphere had been revealed, and the earth's area doubled; a body of land greater than Europe and Africa combined had been laid open to mankind. The way, not to the East, but to the greater West had been discovered.

VI. THE NEW WORLD

THE sun rose, and the men crowding the taffrail looked out at the land-fall. They saw blue water, blue like turquoise, in its depths, and shading shallower into emerald, toward the white sand beach. Beyond that, trees of a foliage greener than they had conceived possible, masked the land's interior. Presently, they saw groups of naked people, "neither black nor white," gathering on the beach.

> " . . . He went ashore in the armed boat and took the royal standard, and Martin-Alonso and Vincent Yanez, his brother, who was captain of the Nina. . . . Presently many of the inhabitants assembled. . . ."

In their minds there was no doubt as to their location. They had sailed for the Indies; the Indies they believed they had found. If the land they saw were the mainland, then it must be the territory of Cathay itself; if an island,

146

then surely one of the twelve thousand seven hundred that Marco Polo reported, along the Indian shore.

But it was, as we now know, none of these: neither Cypango, treasure-land of gold, nor Aprositos, the Inaccessible Isle of the ancients. It was one of the Bahamas—perhaps Watling's Island, or some other of that tiny archipelago lying just east of Cuba—there is no way of determining definitely now.

However, the small-boat touched shore; the Admiral and his captains leaped to the beach, while the islanders stared, astonished. Prayers were said, and praise given for their deliverance. Then, while he held aloft the royal standard, the new Vice-Regent and Governor-General, Lord Admiral of the Ocean Sea, in the name of the Kings, took formal possession of his domain, christening it San Salvador. Rodrigo de Escovedo, notary to the King, made record officially of the act. This done, the members of the group saluted Christopher, "thanking and praising him, and calling him by his title of Vice-Regent and Admiral."

Meanwhile, the natives had watched the ceremony with childish curiosity. When, at last, Columbus turned his attention to his new-found subjects, they proved to be docile and easily conciliated.

"So that they might hold us in friendly feeling," he wrote in his report to the Kings, "and because I felt it would be easier to subjugate them and convert them to our holy faith by kindness and persuasion rather than by violence, I gave them some red caps and glass beads which they hung around their necks, and many other things of slight value, which pleased them greatly, delighting them so much that it was truly a marvel to see . . ."

Their appearance, too, was no less marvellous. Strong, thickset and short of stature, broad-cheeked and flat of forehead, they formed a type unlike any these mariners had ever seen. Their hair, sometimes cut short, sometimes left flowing, was straight and coarse, "like the hairs of a horse's tail." Their bodies were painted, "some black, some white, others red and others what colors they may find: some painting the face and others the whole body, some only around the eyes." As to the natural color of their skin, it was puzzling and difficult to describe—a kind of copper color.

Savages they were, ignorant of the use of iron, arming themselves with reed rods, carrying a whale's tooth for a spearhead. They lived in primitive huts of woven branches, instead of the palaces, tiled with gold, which the explorers had expected.

But of their good will, there could be no doubt. "They came to the ship's boats afterward, swimming and bringing us parrots, skeins of cotton thread, darts—what they had. . . ." Innocent and child-like, it was apparent that the savages believed the Spaniards to be in some way more

148

than mortal visitors. They kissed their hands and feet, and prostrated themselves before them. And these, still flushed with joy at their deliverance and bewildered by the beauties of the paradise on which they had fallen, were gracious and gentle in return.

Next morning, a swarm of canoes paddled out to the anchored vessels—"small boats, made out of the trunk of a tree, all in one piece and very wonderfully made, which they paddle, going at a marvellous speed." More gifts were made, from one to another, and bargains struck. Many were seen to wear small rings, or beaten disks of gold hanging from their ears and nostrils. Questioned, they pointed to the south, making signs which the Spaniards took to mean that in that direction they would find a king who had a store of gold.

Next day, then, the search began. The vessels cruised from island to island, hunting this prince and his treasure. Everywhere they went, the same natural beauties awaited them: "bright green trees, so as to be a pleasure to look on: gardens of the most beautiful trees . . ." deep forests, brilliant in foliage, with "trees very unlike those of our country . . . all of different shape, and so that it is the greatest wonder in the world to see the diversity."

Everywhere the impenetrable, abundant forest, peopled with the brown savages, all naked, men and women alike, who came laughing and bounding like puppies to greet

149

THE LANDING.

"A swarm of canoes paddled out to the anchored vessels—'small boats, made out of the trunk of a tree, all in one piece and very wonderfully made, which they paddle, going at a marvellous speed'."

the strange white divinities. Gifts were given them—
strange, sweet-smelling woods, rare great tropic flowers,
birds of all plumages, parrots, perrokeets, all screeching
and crying in their curious ways.

Everywhere the same blue waters, alive with fish "so
unlike ours that it is wonderful . . . and of the brightest
colors, so that there is not a man who would not be as-
tounded, and would not take great delight in seeing them."
Everywhere a paradise of beauty and diversity—but no
gold.

They cruised here and there among the islands and the
coral reefs. At each island they landed, taking formal possession in the name of the Kings, naming one in honor
of the Virgin Mary, and others *Isabella, Fernandina,
Juana,* after the Queen, the King, and the Crown Prince.

They had brought seven Indians with them from San
Salvador to act as guides and interpreters. With these,
they questioned the natives at each of their landings. But
nowhere did they find the clue that would lead them to the
treasures they sought. Each island, to be sure, had its
king, or *cacique*. But these rulers lacked by far the magnificence of the Grand Khan. Nude, rude and primitive,
their palaces were huts; their courts were held in palm
tree clearings. The gold they possessed was negligible,
consisting chiefly of small ornaments, or strips beaten
thin, and shaped to the form of masks.

They touched a larger body of land, which the natives called Cuba, and which the Admiral re-christened "The Garden of the Queen," in honor of Isabella. And now, at last, they began to think they had found Cypango, or perhaps even the very shore of Asia itself. To make sure, Columbus sent Rodrigo de Jerez and the official interpreter Luis de Torre to explore the interior, and seek out the residence of the Grand Khan, and deliver to him the letter of greeting from the Kings.

Though these messengers failed to discover the palace of that potentate, they witnessed something almost as astonishing: at one of the villages they had visited, the naives were provided with a kind of leaf, which they rolled "into the form of a musket-barrel, but very much smaller," and then, lighting the end, they drew smoke from these into their mouths and blew it forth again, in a manner which showed clearly that the practice gave them pleasure and no harm. The leaf, they discovered, was from a plant which the natives called *tabacos*.

So they wandered from island to island, vainly hunting. If ever the ships' prows had been turned to the northward, little more than a day's sailing would have brought them to Key West and Florida, and the shores of the continent. But the tales the Indians told of the golden lands to the eastward proved a stronger lure for their imaginations, and especially for that of Pinzon.

He it was that was most bitterly disappointed. Columbus had at least justified his honor, and won a Governorship and a Vice-Regency. But he who had sailed as a simple ship's captain had achieved neither title nor wealth. Disgruntled at this failure, and urged on by his natural impatience of character, he decided to steal a march on Christopher. Suddenly, one day, the *Pinta* weighed anchor and disappeared, sailing for Haiti. A fortnight later the Admiral, with the other vessels, came to the same mooring.

This time, no one doubted that they had at last discovered their treasure island. Once again, the ceremony on the beach was performed. The island was named *Española*—Little Spain—and formally added to the possession of the Crown, under the Governorship of Don Christopher, High Admiral of the Ocean Sea. By the same act, a million or more natives of the island came, all unknowing, under the sway of the Most Christian Rulers. The explorers found them as childish and as primitive as the others they had seen. Their towns lay hid in the forest, grouped around the central hut of the *cacique*, which boasted three rooms, for the master, the wives, and one for the mummied bodies of the king's ancestors.

These people had no gold, nor any need for it. They fed on the fish of the sea, and the abundant fruits of the tropic. They had no needs that nature did not meet, no fears, except the occasional incursions of the man-eating Caribs from the neighboring islands.

But the Spaniards found gold dust, and nuggets—few of them, and small in weight, but still gold—in the river-sands, and the dried beds of the streams. And the hunt pushed on, frantically now, for winter was approaching— the men, from every rise and at every turning, straining for sight of the jewelled Asiatic lands they were seeking. "May our Holy Savior, in His pity," wrote Christopher in his journal, "direct me truly, that I may discover the gold we search for!"

Winter had come, forcing them to return to Spain. The land they had discovered had proved to be an Arcadia too complete; it was almost ignorant of gold. But they still had hopes. If they returned home now it would be for new supplies and new provision, to resume the search for Tartary and Cathay.

So, before leaving, a small fort was built, christened *Navidad*—The Nativity—on a site near the region which the natives said would be most rich in gold. The members of the King's Commission, because to leave others would weaken the ships' complement, remained as garrison. A left-hand relative of Christopher—Diego de Arana, neph-ew of Beatriz Enriquez—was given the command of the little troupe.

The return voyage began with a misfortune. Hardly

out of the harbor, the *Santa-Maria* struck on a sand-reef and was lost. The crew and the Admiral, however, were saved. Christopher took command of the *Nina.* The little fleet, now one-third diminished, continued out of these waters of their discovery, sailing homeward, toward the east.

They had seen strange lands and stranger peoples. They had widened the stretch of man's geographical knowledge by two thousand miles. If they had found no gold, nor any of the pearls, jewels, spices, silks and magnificence they had set out for, they still felt they had been always on the threshold of that discovery. So, in the happiest hope for the future, they followed the ocean track for Palos. Of the great continent of America, that stretched its ridged mountains and wide plains, its ice fields, swamp lands, deep rivers and mighty forests—of that continent, lying like a sleeping giant across their path, they had no faintest idea.

As the outward voyage had been pleasant, with still seas and gentle winds, so now was the return difficult. It almost seemed as if the sailors' apprehensions had been justified; breezes were all contrary, "having great trouble with the wind, high and tempestuous seas . . ." The Journal is of a continual battle with the elements.

The wind moderated from time to time, but always "in-

155

creased again . . . during the night the waves were terrible, rising against each other and so shaking and straining the *Nina* that she was in danger of being stove in. . . . Sunrise, the wind blew harder . . . we reefed the mainsail close . . . finally we began to run before the wind, there being nothing else to do . . . the cross seas were terrific . . . the *Pinta*, with Martin-Alonso, out of sight; although we kept showing lanterns all night, and they answered us. . . ."

On the twelfth of February—they were nearing home; just off the Azores—it seemed as if Fate had withheld its heaviest blow to the last—the tempest reached its maximum. The great winds and violent seas seemed to come from all sides, the two tiny vessels travelling always at the center of the hurricane.

Pandemonium aboard the ships. The men vowed a pilgrimage to the shrines of Our Lady of Guadalupe, Our Lady of Loretta, to Santa Maria of Magliera, if they were saved—and drew lots to see who should accomplish it, while the storm raged. The ships drove on, the bows whipping to all points of the compass, "the mainsail close-reefed, so the vessel might rise to the waves: otherwise she would have been swamped."

And the storm continued. The sailors, fearing that they had been too niggardly with the Virgin before, made another and collective vow, to go, in shirts and barefoot, to

give thanks in the first port they reached. The seven Indians, taken first as guides, brought now as trophies, knelt
on the poop-deck, endlessly repeating the *Salve* their new
masters had taught them.

Meanwhile, the two captains acted according to their different temperaments. Martin-Alonso, whose nature, itself
tempestuous, welcomed the hurricane, now sought to turn
the storm to serve his own ends. Hoping to evade, if not
completely to lose, his rival and commander, he took advantage of the Pinta's faster sailing and made away, for
Spain.

Christopher had a weightier concern than even his own
ambitions. For himself, he might well die, and gratefully.
But if he perished, the secret of the western lands, all
the fruit of his discovery, would die with him. Accordingly, while the wind howled and the men ran above deck,
he went down to his cabin and there wrote off the history
of his voyage, tracing the path he had taken, and declar-
ing that these lands he had discovered had been formally
taken in the name of the Crown of Spain. This done, he
rolled the document in waxed paper, sealed it with wax,
and enclosed it—with a note promising one thousand ducats to the finder, if he would carry it to the Queen—in a
small barrel, which he cast into the sea. "All the men,"
he says, "believed it to be some act of devotion."

Soon after, the wind changed, and the sea became

calmer; they sailed before it. That night, some of the men saw a light, to leeward. Next day, they dropped anchor in the port of Santa Maria, in the Azores. The *Pinta* had disappeared.

True to their vows, some of the crew went in procession to visit the altar of the Virgin. They were halted by the Portuguese Governor of the town, because of the proscription against the Admiral. It was only with the greatest difficulty that Christopher was able to obtain their freedom, and continue. And again they met with storms, so that at last they were forced to seek shelter in Lisbon harbor, on the very hearth of his enemies.

Immediately, he sent letters to King John II, of Portugal, to the Court of Spain, to Luis de Santangel, and the Chancellor Don Raphael Sanchez, stating that he had discovered the Indies, and had safely returned. There was a pardonable pride in all this. Eleven years before, in debt and bare of all possesions, he had left this town of Lisbon, to which he now returned, an Admiral and a conqueror. He demanded that he be greeted by the officers of the port with all the ceremony due his rank, and so he re-entered the city, to the sound of drums and trumpets. The welcome, however, did not diminish the resentment which the King felt toward him.

Christopher's success was a blow both to that ruler's pride and his interest. He adopted the policy which Mach-

iavelli was soon to recommend as the diplomacy of kings.
He dissembled. The Admiral was invited to Val-Paradiso,
the summer palace; there the monarch greeted him most
courteously, paid him many signal honors, not the least
being that he was permitted to be seated, and remain covered in the royal presence, while he recounted the details
of his marvellous journey.

Later, while the King's most distinguished officers conducted Christopher on a visit to the royal gardens, the
King's councillors met to deliberate on the fate that was
to be meted out to him. A great number of the ministers
were in favor of death. The punishment, they argued,
was well merited: had he not, on at least two occasions,
ignored or directly disobeyed the royal command? This
was treason. Moreover—to come to the nub of the matter—to kill him now would be, in great measure, to destroy the value of his discoveries. Lacking his leadership,
the Spanish Crown must move blindfold in the matter.
Portugal might still claim the West.

The argument was well received. Several courtiers
eagerly sought the honor and privilege of killing the unwelcome foreigner.

And so once more the destiny of the Genoese adventurer
hung by the slenderest of threads. How easy a matter it
would have been, in those unruly days, to dispose of him
thus. "You jostled me, sir!" some foppish gentleman

would have said, as he passed along a corridor. "Are your feet clods, that you must tread on my toes?" as he waited in an antechamber. Then the sword that he had by birth no right to wear would have proved his undoing. A meeting, outside the city walls; a thrust or two; a grave ready-dug and quickly filled; a little whispering, later, in the palace—this would have marked the end of his career.

Martin-Alonso, most of all, would have profited by the event. There would have been no Admiral to outshine him at the Spanish Court. History hates uncertainties; with the passing of time, his fame would have been the brighter as Columbus' fate remained obscure. Quite possibly, the rough and greedy old fisherman of Palos might have come to be regarded as one of the great figures of his age.

However, Christopher's uneven destiny had not yet run its course. He had still much to endure: many voyages, many triumphs, much bitterness. Tempted sorely by the logic of his councillors, King John nevertheless decided against so brutal an assassination. The commerce of the sea was the life of Portugal, and that commerce would be hurt irreparably by such an outrage against its code. He dared not violate the hospitality he owed to a ship-wrecked mariner.

So Christopher, returned from his promenade through the garden walks, with many smiles and bows was ushered into the Presence again, and received graciously. The Queen greeted him. The gentlemen all saluted him. The King himself gave him God-speed to Castille.

At noon, on the fifteenth of March, 1493, Columbus dropped anchor in the harbor of Palos, after seven months lacking twelve days of navigation.

Such a town, whose ships like its children go forth to the sea, always greets their return with joy. But the *Nina* came back like a prodigal, long lost and long unhoped for, and the sight of her salt-roughened timbers, her patched, and tattered sails, sent the whole population into a kind of delirium of welcome. All the hates, the spites, the fears, the petty avarices that had surrounded his departure were forgotten in a moment. The town adopted him, his glory, his success. And their minds stirred eagerly, at thought of the far countries he had come from.

Shoeless and in sack-cloth, Christopher climbed the slope to the monastery above the town, and knelt to give thanks to Our Lady of La Rabida. Followed a happy reunion with the friends of his friendless days, the Prior Juan Perez, Father Antonio and the other Franciscans. Soon after, he departed for Seville.

Here a letter from the Kings awaited him. They greeted him as "Our Admiral of the Ocean Sea, Vice-Regent and Governor of the islands discovered in the Indies," congratulated him on the happy outcome of his enterprise and commanded him immediately to Barcelona, where the Court lay. He hastened, naturally, to obey.

His progress through the land had now assumed something of the proportions of a triumphal march, and one as gaudy, gay and variegated perhaps as the world had seen since the Roman emperors came home from their victories. Leading all, rode the Admiral, his face weatherworn and his hair graying; he wore the robe of a Franciscan Brother, but his guard bore breast-plate, pike and spur. Behind him came his servants and valetry, with the long train of his trophies. Here one bears aloft a bundle of bamboo reeds, the long, sharp-pointed leaves shaking to the march. Others carry parrots, red, green and yellow, screaming in their cages; others, a crocodile, stuffed and mounted, or branches of strange woods, or the implements of the Indians.

So the strange caravan winds slowly across the countryside. At every chapel, Christopher enters, to make his devotions before the altar. At every wayside cross, prayers are said, and the seven Indians brought back with him cross themselves with the sign of the cross. And everywhere, all along the way there is rejoicing and wonderment, the whole populace gathering to celebrate the passing of these voyagers, returning from their magical voyage.

162

So through the rocky wastes of Castille, and the flowered fields of Aragon, and on to Barcelona. The welcome of the Sovereigns was as whole-hearted as that of their subjects, though more formal. He kissed their hands, in token of loyalty, then the seat of honor, next the throne, was given him. Through all the solemnities of the interview, great deference was paid him. At the end, the whole assemblage knelt, singing the *Te Deum*.

On the twentieth of March, 1493, the Kings delivered to him his letters of nobility. The escutcheon devised for him bore, in the first quartering, the castle of Castille; in the second, the lion of Leon; in the third, a wave, azure, sown with islands, or; the field of the fourth quartering was left vacant, according to the tradition, "to be occupied by the arms you were accustomed to bear."

This last reservation proved no small embarrassment to the newly created nobleman. Hitherto, he had used to good purpose the similarity of his name to that of the Colombos of higher birth. Their arms were known, of course, to the heralds: the Colombos of Cuccaro bore three doves, argent, on a field of azure; those of Piacenza, a stalk, in argent. Some one of these, he knew, was expected of him.

However, he dared not counterfeit so openly and irrevocably. Eventually, he foreswore the symbolical charges and presented to the learned Heralds a coat-of-arms so fantastic in its blazonry as to fill them with astonishment: "a band of azure cutting diagonally from right to left across a field of gold, with a chief of gules," was the fashion in which he described it.

The Province of Aragon, it will be remembered, had had no share in the financing of Columbus' expedition. Now, deprived of its profits, it might feel a certain envy of the conqueror, so that the Aragonese author of the *Dietaria* of Barcelona is found, in his entry for the day of Christopher's arrival in the city, to make no mention of him in his journal. And there might be others who brooded at the honors showered on the *parvenu*. Nevertheless, the Admiral remained the hero of the day.

It might be pointed out that, if the expedition had been a triumph, it had been remarkably meager of material profit. It might be asked if he had found the Indies why had he not brought back its treasure. Nevertheless, Christopher's eloquence, and his own conviction, prevailed. The Florentine, Tribaldo de Rossi, a shrewd observer of events, commented in his journal that, "the King of Spain took greater joy at the Admiral's return than he did at the conquest of Granada."

And certainly Christopher had great hopes, if little gold, to offer. It remained now to realize on them. The work of outfitting a fleet was begun at Cadiz. In Seville, the or-

164

ganization of an administrative body, to govern the new-found colonies, was started.

At the head of this "Indian Ministry," the Kings placed Don Juan Rodriguez de Fonseca, Arch-Deacon of Burgos. Though a churchman, this gentleman was considered an excellent executive as well. His manner was a study in paradox. Grave to the point of solemnity, a disorder of the nerves would set him twitching like St. Vitus' dance. Strict and severe in the cathedral, his castle at Coca, near Segovia, was noted for the luxury of its appointments.

Meanwhile, at Seville, the Kings and their Councillors, aided by Don Juan de Fonseca, were busy promulgating the laws which were to govern the provinces. The fact that they knew nothing of these regions, neither their size, their climate, nor their population, hardly troubled them. They held close to the traditional principles on which the power of Spain was based. Heresy must be obliterated, and the inhabitants converted to the Catholic faith. The privilege of emigration and colonization was reserved to the natives of Castille. The monopoly of trade and commerce was given, by natural right, to the Crown.

And now, as preparations progressed for the second expedition, all Spain exulted. All, that is, except two. One was Martin-Alonso. While Columbus made harbor at Palos, Pinzon had landed in Galicia, never doubting that he was the sole surviving officer of the expedition. Profiting by this circumstance, he made haste to report to the Kings. His disappointment, when he learned the truth, was as great as had been his ambitions before. The hardy mariner, who had weathered so many storms, was conquered at last by his own stormy temper. He died, almost literally of spite, at the Admiral's triumph.

The other malcontent was the sailor, Rodrigo Triana, who claimed to have first sighted land. In spite of his claims, however, the honor—and with it the pension of ten thousand maravedis—was awarded by the Queen to Columbus, on the ground that he had sighted the shore earlier, when he pointed out the light in the darkness to Pero Guttierez and the others.

Triana disappeared. It is said that he took his grievances to Africa, foreswore the Christian faith and joined with Arabs. Whatever his fate. nothing more was ever heard of him.

If Christopher's pretensions to noble birth may seem occasionally, in this day, to savor somewhat of snobbery, it can never be argued, however, that he was as ungrateful and unfilial as the true snob generally is. The sense of family in him was strong; it was not dulled by his successes. Bartholomew, of course, was already well placed, in the service of Madame de Bourbon. When the news of Christopher's triumph reached the Court of France, Charles

VIII called Bartholomew before him to hear the account, rewarded him with a purse of one hundred crowns, and sent him on his way to Seville.

Of the other brothers, Giovanni-Pellegrino was dead, Giacomo, the delicate, was still alive and living at Genoa. He had, in the year 1484, at the age of sixteen, entered as apprentice in the shop of Lucchino Cadamartori, master weaver at .Savona. According to the agreement, he had undertaken to serve faithfully for twenty-two months, offering his clothing, even to the shirts he wore, as guarantee. In exchange, his master agreed to provide him, at the term of his duties, with a pair of shoes, and woollen trousers, and a cloak of fustian. Apparently his apprenticeship had been satisfactory; in 1492 he was employed, like his brother before him, as a wool-carder at Genoa.

Christopher, learning his whereabouts, called him immediately to Seville, and made him his aide. There is something touching in the picture thus presented, of the young and horny-handed Italian laborer finding his fustian cloak suddenly supplanted by the satin-weave of the Court.

Meanwhile, preparations were being made at the Cathedral to baptize the seven Indians. In the pomp of the ceremony, Christopher perceived an excellent occasion to present his brother to the Kings. In the opinion of those expert in the dogma of the day, none other than the Admiral could be considered as the preceptor of the natives in the

Faith. Accordingly, it.was arranged that the King and the Infante would be god-fathers to all but two of them; Giacomo was signally honored by the same office for these.

And so the dream voyage ended, like a dream. All Spain and its people swam in the delight of its accomplishment. The seven Indians, still bewildered, were gratified by the gift of necklaces and other trinkets, from their god-fathers. Giacomo Columbus, abandoning forever his looms, forsook at the same time the name his plebeian parents had given him; he was rechristened Diego. A number of gilded and courtly personages found themselves suddenly installed in fat sinecures over-seas, and armed themselves with sheaves of paper and bundles of quill-pens for the exercise of their office. Ferdinand augmented his titles by that of King of the Indies.

And Christopher, at last, overwhelmed with praise, laden with honors, drowned in adulation—did he not sometimes rub his eyes and turn dizzy at the heights to which he had risen? Was it not, perhaps, all a dream? He pinched himself, half expecting to awaken in the squalor of the *via del Mulcento*, with his father's wine-tuns around him, and before him his loom, and perhaps, filtering in through the window, a gust of the salt breeze from the familiar port.

168

VII. GOLD FROM THE INDIES

T HE miracle of miracles had happened; it remained now to coin its profits. Until now, the right of possession by discovery had never been questioned. Nevertheless, to preserve such an important acquisition every precaution must be taken. The Kings, therefor, applied to Rome for Pontifical confirmation in their El Dorado. They received three Bulls in reply.

The first, an *Inter Cetera* dated May third, 1493, praised the Sovereigns for their work in exploration and the propagation of the Faith, and invested them with sovereignty over all the lands discovered in the west.

By the second, *Eximie Devotionis*, the Pontiff upheld their right to possession of "all the continents and islands distant and unknown, lying in the western regions, in the Ocean Sea, which have been or shall be discovered by you or by your efforts, providing they be not already under the rule of a Christian prince."

The third, another *Inter Cetera,* dated May fourth, stated: "You have sent our son in the Faith, Christopher Columbus, a good and courageous man by more than one reckoning, and well worthy to command so great an enterprise, with ships and the men necessary, to search out the western lands, and the islands lying far and unknown . . . in a sea whereon until now no man had ever sailed. And these men, with the help of God, have discovered certain of these far islands, and continents which no other had ever discovered. . . ."

Proceeding further, the bull established the famous line of demarcation, giving possession to Spain of all lands they might discover to the west of an imaginary line drawn from pole to pole, at the distance of one hundred leagues to the west of the Azores and the Cape Verde Islands. To the eastward, all discoveries belonged to Portugal. This reservation of all the fruits of exploration to two nations alone did not, naturally, prove pleasant to the rest. Later, Francis I of France was to ask with irony which new codicil to Adam's will had been found, to disinherit the other Christian nations.

But news, when Alexander Borgia thus summarily sliced the globe in two, still travelled slow. It was a long time before the results of Christopher's voyage became known throughout Europe. Kings had word of it from their agents to other courts; the great traders had the reports of their branches abroad. The dilettante would buy and read the pamphlet which some enterprising printer, eventually, would issue in chronicle of the event. To the general public, the news came, much later, through the slow and twisted channels of rumor.

The first printed report of the discovery came in 1493: a four-page pamphlet in-folio, issued by Pedro Posa at Barcelona, containing the text of Columbus' letter to Santangel, Secretary to the King. Soon after, Leandro de Cosco translated into Latin the letter to Raphael Sanchez, Chancellor of the Exchequer, issuing it under the title: "The Letter of Christopher Columbus—to whom our age is much indebted—concerning the Indian Islands recently discovered, in the Indies, beyond the River Ganges, in the search for which he was sent eight months ago at the charge and expense of the Most Powerful King Ferdinand of Spain: this letter addressed to Raphael Sanxis, Treasurer of the said King, and translated from Spanish into Latin by the noble and learned Aliander de Cosco."

The same text was reprinted in April, 1493, by Stephanus Planck, and later by seven other printers, variously of Rome, Paris, Basle and Anvers. It was not until 1497 that the first German edition appeared; at about the same time a Florentine monk, Guiliano Dati, issued an Italian translation, in verse.

Kings and princes sought eagerly for all the news that

could be had, concerning the discovery. The Duke Hercule d'Este wrote to his ambassadors at Florence, commanding him to inquire of Maestro Lodovico, nephew and heir of Paolo Toscanelli, now dead, if there remained among the Doctor's papers any further information about the western islands.

Outside the courts and chancelleries, the news found interest in other quarters as well. Cartographers, cosmographers and amateurs of the arts were eager for information to revise their charts. Traders, importers and exporters, ships' captains and ship-builders wondered how far and in what way it would affect their affairs. Pharmacists, druggists, chemists and perfumers waited impatiently for the new oils and essences that would surely soon be put on the market.

Men of the arts, too, were affected by the drama of the undertaking, those of the Humanist School especially, for had not one of their number, and the best-beloved, been in some measure the instigator of the voyage? So Pomponio Leto, at the report, burst into tears of joy. With others, the tears dripped from their pens, and a deluge of odes, epistles and commemoratory poems in weighty Latin meter was let loose in honor of the new-day Argonauts.

Nevertheless, and oddly, the impact of the triumph did not reach to the common mass. Genoa, his birthplace, was perhaps too far away to be affected, and in Spain, Christopher was still an exile from the native folk-lore: he could not replace the *Cid*. Perhaps, to be a common hero, one must fight with common things, and Columbus' achievement was too mystic in its quality and too general in its effect to dominate the popular mind. He had opened new lands, but only to seize them for the Crown; he promised wealth, but for the coffers of the Kings. And the people, once the flourish of his arrival was silenced, soon forgot him, reserving their folk-songs and balladry for the knight who might combat their local dragons and destroy them.

However, if the taverns overlooked him, Christopher was still the center of interest at the Court and at Barcelona. The Duke of Medina-Sidonia, so cold before, now offered five million maravedis toward the second expedition. To supply the remainder, the confiscated properties of Jews and heretics, banished by the Crown, were sold. With the capital thus acquired, Juanoto Berardi, shipbuilder at Cadiz, equipped seventeen ships for the voyage.

The Kings proclaimed again the titles and appointments of the Admiral, confirming him in his privileges. He then took his departure, going to Seville, where he supervised the final preparations for the expedition.

How changed now were his circumstances, since the days at Palos! There, to get even three small caravels, he met with ridicule and defiance, greed and hate; to get a crew, he had to drum them out of taverns, and swell the list with a complement of convicts, at the end. Now, the shoe was on the other foot: he it was who had to hide from the swarms of seekers. Sailors, adventurers, traders, financiers greedy of gold, outfitters, ships' captains, noblemen offering their swords for a share in the booty—all were burning, begging, crying for a chance to sail with him to the new El Dorado, the Islands of Gold!

When at last, on September 20, 1493, the seventeen vessels weighed anchor and sailed out of the port of Cadiz, they were laden with a troupe of fifteen hundred men, enlisted beneath the banner of the Admiral. Adventurers all, they came from all classes—professional soldiers, tradesmen, craftsmen; even the Church was represented, by the Abbot of Luzerna.

Christopher, looking back from the *Maria-Galanta,* his flagship, saw his sons Diego and Fernando, waving from the pierside. A year ago, the one had been with the monks of Rabida, the other was sharing the poverty of Beatriz. Now, thanks to his triumph, he saw both of them, resplendent in their uniform as pages of the Infante Don Juan. And if that first voyage, so poorly fitted, so ill prepared for the enterprise, had brought him such success, what then would be his triumph now, with an army and a flotilla at his command? So he watched the shoreline fade and vanish, and turned to lay his course into the west.

174

The first leg of the voyage, as before, took them to the Canaries. Here they took on food and supplies for the journey before them, buying, among others, eight pigs, to be introduced on the western shores. Unlike the human colonists who joined them, these animals were destined to multiply enormously. Every barnyard and packing house, today, owes a debt to Columbus.

And then, leaving the Canaries, the great fleet embarked on the western waters. With the wind behind them, and all sails set, prows creaming and the wake boiling astern, they drove on into the west. All eyes turned in that direction, and every eye had the same vision before it—gold!

Columbus' glance, too, had the same gleam to entice it, though less dazzled by its ray. His journeys with the Centurione had taught him how rare the metal was, how essential it was to the life of trade, how powerful the man would be who could control it. As the taste for luxury extended, the greed for the gold which alone could gratify those luxuries grew more acute, until now prince and pauper alike were vassals under its dominion.

He knew, too, how low the treasury of his royal patrons had gone, and how great their indebtedness. He knew how much his fleet had cost and where it had been borrowed. And he knew that it had all been done with one purpose and one understanding—that he would come back with gold—gold to repay their creditors, gold to fit out armies

175

for new conquests; gold for the generals and gold for the cathedrals, that the might, the prestige and the piety of the Crown might be maintained.

So seen, each one of the vessels that followed behind him in his fleet became an added obligation on his shoulders. He was no longer an adventurer, with little funds and small equipment, seeking out distant places and far lands to confirm an opinion or justify an Idea. The very magnitude of his undertaking had launched him now as a trader, a kind of knight-errant of finance, and gold was the Grail he sought.

The winds were kind, stronger, if possible, and steadier than before. Twenty days sufficed for the journey. On the third of November, one of the pilots on the *Maria-Galanta* gave the cry: *"Tenemos tierra!"*—"We have the land!"

The landfall was among the Caribbean Islands, the largest of which they christened *Guadalupe*. Some time later, toward the end of the month, the flotilla anchored off the shore of Española. Two guns were fired, and the ships' complement crowded to the rails, watching the beach and waiting for a reply from the bombards in the fort of La Navidad. They waited in vain.

Landing, they went to the fort's emplacement. They found there the ashes of the walls, the broken and flame-blackened rafters lying in ruin, already choked by the jungle growth. Searching further, Christopher discovered

176

the bodies of his old companions, scorched and rotting; they had been tied by the hands to wooden crosses, choked with grass-rope, and burned.

Later, they learned the tragic history of the little garrison. It would seem that the natives, who had first believed them to be gods, had early discovered their mistake. The gentlemen of the King's commission, for all their learning, had not proved immune to the charms of the opposite sex; each had amply wived himself, with four or five of the native girls, and had shown small respect for the customs, either of their own or the new land, in the process.

Subsequently, they began the hunt for gold. Now, if for these simple savages the metal had no commercial value, it was nevertheless, by their religion, invested with certain mystic qualities which the Spaniards, probably neither knowing nor caring, had outraged. According to the native faith, the hunt for gold could be undertaken only under certain conditions, chief of which was that of chastity.

The signal failure of the garrison in this observance brought the natives to revolt, and the Spaniards, divided by jealousies and petty differences, were not able to resist. They were completely overwhelmed, killed, and with their death was also destroyed the awe in which the whites had been held before.

Columbus broke ground, not far from the site of La

177

Navidad, for a new city, naming it Isabella. Here, while he waited to organize the hunt for gold in the interior, he laid out fields and began their cultivation. In that climate, food grew ripe for the picking. Life was easy and fecund. The Spaniards settled in their little Paradise, with few troubles and no fears, save for the crocodiles which haunted the river-beds—strange, flat-jawed, dragon-shaped monsters which, the natives said, attacked by sticking the pointed tail in the ground and hurling themselves forward by the leverage.

There was one other danger which was longer in developing.

The question of the origin of syphilis is a much-discussed one, and the disease is often maintained to have been indigenous to the West Indian natives, and by them transmitted to the Spaniards.

It is known, however, that already in 1493 the disease had appeared in France, ravaging Paris to such an extent that Charles VIII sent criers through the town, ordering all so infected to leave the city, "soubs peine d'estre jectez en la rivière"—under penalty of being drowned in the river. Those who elected to flee were compelled to have their names registered against a return, at the city gates; they were then provided each with a purse of four *sols* to carry them on their way. The slums of Spain were probably no more free from the contagion than those of France.

178

It is quite likely, therefor, that the men of the first garrison at La Navidad had the infection among them. The peculiar susceptibility of primitive peoples to the disease is well known; once transmitted, it spread with greater rapidity and virulence. The men of the second expedition paid with usury for the sins of the first.

So the germ, once transplanted, flourished with tropical exuberance, and the legend of its origin in the west, first stated by Ulrich von Hutten, was perpetuated by the chronicler Oviedo. It is, however, more or less certain that the wide dissemination of the disease, continuing to our day, dates from the excursions made by the Admiral's adventurers out from the town of Isabella to the women of the native villages nearby. Returning to Europe afterward, many of them enlisted in the Neapolitan Wars; infecting the camp-followers of their own army, these in turn transmitted it to the French; thus begun it passed rapidly throughout the world. It was known during the succeeding centuries as the "French Disease," or the "Neapolitan Sickness." Had they known, Columbus' fifteen hundred might have feared it more than the crocodiles.

While his men were so occupied, Christopher undertook his first shipment home. It was made up of aromatic woods, bark and herbs and other natural products, for the most part, and consisted of ten caravels. It sailed under the command of Antonio de Torre, brother to the governess of the Infante Don Juan, to whom Columbus also intrusted a letter addressed to the Kings.

In this, the new Vice-Regent revealed a lively interest in the success of his colony and its subjects. At the same time, paradoxically, his concern found outlet in a suggestion itself the seed of the major misfortunes which were to afflict them. The letter recommended that the colonists be permitted to import from Spain each year "good herds of cattle and livestock," to be paid for "in slaves, taken among the cannibals who, though ferocious of character, are strong, able, soundly built and of considerable intelligence, so that once they had been cured of their habitual cruelty they would be more valuable than any other kind of slave."

There was, of course, nothing inhuman or revolting in this suggestion, to the eye of the century in which Columbus lived. Men were the common plunder of victory; the conqueror owned the life of his captive. If the captive were a Christian, he could buy himself back again, by paying ransom; if an infidel, he was sold, willy-nilly, to someone else. So, during the Moorish Wars, all captives went under the system of *repartimientos*: divided in three lots and sold, the proceeds of the first third went to ransom Christian prisoners, the second to the officers, and the third to the royal treasury. Christopher himself remembered the auction blocks in the market-place of Genoa, where the

Tartar and Circassian maidens were sold to gratify the luxurious tastes of the patricians.

It was natural, then, that he should suggest this means to increase the royal revenue form the colony. Spain itself was already full of slaves, some retained from the Arab Wars, some bought through Portugal, from Africa. Nevertheless, perhaps out of deference to the scruples of the Queen, he was careful to suggest only the enslavement of the cannibals.

For the moment, however, the Kings took no action in the matter. Their reply allowed all his other requests, and appointed Don Juan de Fonseca to superintend their execution.

During this interchange, the situation with respect to his fifteen hundred followers was becoming acute. In accordance with their articles of enlistment, the sailors, the actual ships' crews were alone entitled to salary. The others, soldiers and adventurers, came without pay and at their own expense, with the hope of gold for their regard. Such men, naturally, had little interest in the slow work which the founding of a solid colony entails. In their lively imaginations, they had pictured themselves as stepping ashore when the voyage ended, to pick up gold nuggets by the hatful, and sail away again, their fortunes made, in a week or so.

Instead, they found themselves set to work hoeing and

shovelling, back-breaking labor, especially under a climate particularly unfavorable. The pressure of their dissatisfaction soon grew so great that the Admiral had to bend before it. He appointed his brother Diego to the command of the fleet, secured all arms and ammunition aboard the *Maria-Galanta*, and then, at the head of his troupe, set out for the interior.

The mines were located at Cibao—"Rocky Hill"—controlled by the *cacique* Caonabo—"The Master of the Golden House." The Spaniards met with little resistance from the natives, who were terrified by their horses, which they imagined to be a two-headed monster, incorporate with the men who rode them. Many came with offerings of roast fowl and other delicacies, hoping to propitiate the beasts. None dared combat them.

The Admiral built and garrisoned a fortress on a hilltop, dominating the mines, and returned to Isabella, resorting to the sea for further exploration. They discovered the island of Jamaica, and coasted along the shores of Cuba. Here they learned from the natives that a great cacique reigned to the westward; his name was Mango.

To Christopher, this was proof positive of his assumption that Cuba was in fact the eastern tip of Asia. Did not every one know that the Province of Mangi lay there, south of Cathay? The Abbot of Luzerna, more cautious, was of another opinion; he imagined that this was no continent they had landed on, but an island.

But the Admiral prevailed, and his view, by the way, was the one accepted by cartographers throughout that and the subsequent century, so that the *Cosmographia* of Munster, issued at the beginning of the seventeenth century, still shows Cuba as a sort of appendage to the continent.

Christopher's obsession, however, had passed the point where it could tolerate dissension, even unspoken. His great Idea, too long deferred of fulfillment, must manufacture proof to satisfy its fever. Accordingly, by order of the Admiral, the notary Fernando Perez de Luna took testimony of all the members of the expedition, affirming that they had arrived on "the continent of the Indies," commanding all who disagreed to declare themselves, under fine of 10,000 maravedis, or one hundred lashes, or the clipping of their tongues, if they should thereafter declare otherwise.

Under such conditions, of course, no one refused. The document was duly drawn, signed and sealed, and sent back to the Court of Spain. The fleet then set sail for Española.

Here a happy surprise awaited Christopher. Three caravels had arrived during his absence; their commander was none other than his beloved brother Bartholomew, now returned to him after an absence of eight years. Christo-

pher immediately appointed him *Adelentado*—Lieutenant-
Governor—of the island. He had another reason to welcome him, beside the sentimental.

His followers, never given over-much to discipline, were
now approaching a state of anarchy. It was impossible to
make them work. Later, Cortez himself was to retort
haughtily to a Governor at Española, "I came here, not
to dig the earth like a peasant, but to seek out gold." It was
but an echo of the cry of Columbus' adventurers.

Many had already deserted, going out in groups of two
or three, or even alone, to wander from village to village
in the forest, seeking by whatever means they could command to find where the treasure lay. The means they used
were sometimes cruel and inhuman; for they refused to
believe that the Indians were ignorant of the secret hiding-
places. At the end, the natives rebelled.

In this, the first native insurrection, the Admiral came
off an easy victor. The revolt was put down. Don Alonzo
de Hojeda, a chevalier of Castille, took captive the *cacique*
Caonabo himself. For ransom, tribute was levied from his
tribe. Each man of fourteen years or over must bring a
kerchief-full of gold dust; lacking this, an equal value of
cotton thread must be provided. Each man, as he brought
his quota, was rewarded with an identifying disk of copper
which he must henceforth wear about his neck; otherwise
he might have his ears cut off, for shirking the payment.

If we are, and no doubt as the Indians were, surprised at the severity of this penalty, it is certain that the white men were not. Such sentences were common enough in Europe at that day. King Henry of Castille ordered the ears to be cut off any man found cutting the trees of his domain, and the penalty was so common for other crimes that when Eustache de la Fosse was caught as a smuggler and brought before the King of Portugal, the monarch's first concern was to inquire whether the ears of his captive had already been clipped. It is probable that most of the colonists thought the defaulting Indians were being treated too easily.

At any rate, discipline continued lax. Christopher did his best to combat the difficulty. The more turbulent were sent back in irons to Spain; the others he treated with severity or persuasion, as the case seemed to demand. His men remained uncontrollable.

In this precarious situation, a ship arrived with a gift which cheered him mightily. It was a contribution from the Queen, toward the outfitting of the vice-royal mansion, in the colony. There were one hundred hens and six roosters, seventy-five pounds of fine soap, ten reams of writing paper, a supply of rose water and orange essence for his hands, a carpet, several tapestry hangings embroidered with trees and flowers, two chests of wood, a bed with two pillows made of fine cloth, six sheets of Holland weave, and bed-covers embroidered with the Admiral's arms—a gift at once regal and womanly.

Christopher was now in his forty-second year of life, and that life had known much adventure and many vicissitudes. All was hardening now, every impulse growing stronger— even those of his weaknesses, every characteristic tightening, tensing, as if in preparation for the hardships he still did not foresee.

His was a nature at once violent and reserved; vigorous, yet with a plaintive confidingness at its core. Instinct, in him, took the place of a more formal education; his only culture was the native refinement and delicacy of the Italian. He loved nature, never failing to comment on a beautiful countryside, remarking the plumage of birds and the aspect of the sea, while he had an almost feminine delight in perfumes and the scent of flowers. Rose and dried orange-leaves were always pressed in with his linen, for their aroma; yet his diet was strict and ascetic, consisting for the most part of dates and rice and similar dishes.

The same strictness ruled his heart. As far as is known, Indian girls and ladies of Seville alike, left him untouched in his later celibate years. His wife was dead, and her memory too. The other, and the one he had most loved, Beatriz, remained in Spain. He had made over to her his pension of ten thousand maravedis, from the Queen.

186

His one excess was his intolerance. There had been long years of poverty, shame and ridicule: he had supported them, kept his temper under control. Now, in his triumph, he was tempted to release the reins and let his anger rise when it moved him. Apart from these moments of violence, however, his general attitude was profound and observant; he was logical of mind, an excellent persuader.

He read much, and exercised a considerable gift for languages. Though he could express himself almost equally in Latin, Spanish and Italian, his customary language was the Castillian; his style was typical of the seaman he was: forceful, animated, swift-flowing. Such writings as he left —his letter of discovery, the log of his voyages, his epistles to the Kings—show a mind vigorous and dramatic, shrewd in reasoning, yet quick to seize the speaking phrase. There is an utter lack of the stilted sentences common to court documents; he tells the tale of his adventures to his sovereigns in much the same free-and-easy fashion as a sailor, yarning with his companions—like those sailors he had heard, when he filled the wine-pitchers for the tables, in the tavern on the *via de Mulcento.*

And if, occasionally, one feels that he strives a little for effect, that his off-hand manner has still its subtle end in view, there remains, nevertheless, one side of his character whose sincerity can not be doubted. From the beginning, all his life had been colored by a kind of mysticism hardly

187

to be defined, but which had drawn him inexorably toward his destiny. That quality found its expression, as the poet in his poems, in his religion.

So he signed his letters and decorated his books with initials, cabalistically arranged:

.S.

.S   .A.   S.
X   M   Y
XPO FERENS

—Enigmas whose meaning has never been solved, save that the last line above, supposedly, means: *Christo Ferens* —"Christ-Bearer," and indicates the religious import of the remainder. Again, sometimes, he concludes a page with the legend taken from the psalms: *Mirabilis elationis maris: mirabilis in altis Dominus*—"Marvellous is the tumult of the waves: marvellous is God on high."

And now, more and more, as his troubles increased, he turned to the consolation of his mystic faith. Now, in the present situation, he found himself at sea, amid a storm of human emotions more uncontrollable than the tempest or the wave. The anarchy of his subordinates was made more dangerous by the trials, both moral and physical, which tropic life imposes on the white man. At home, in Seville, the ministers charged with the affairs of the colonies had shown themselves jealous and obtuse of understanding, vain of their own privileges, and bitter toward his own.

If this had not been enough, it was becoming apparent, even to himself, that the task of organizing and administering so vast an undertaking was beyond his own capacity or experience. He had, by many stipulations, assured himself the Governorship of half the world, and he was gradually coming to understand that he might far better have asked less, and profited more. Even a Centurione or a di Negri, accustomed to mighty enterprise and myriad details, could hardly have weathered such a labyrinth as faced him. Christopher was entrapped immediately, and the more quickly for his own haste.

But he had need of haste. Gold was his aim; he could not manufacture it, he must find where it lay. He must find gold and quickly. He must repay the debts of his undertaking, find gold for the Kings, and the noble gentlemen who were his patrons. He must bring back gold.

It is not children who are most likely to take their fairy-stories seriously. In the pride of his returning, in the splendor of his reception after the first voyage, Christopher had lost his cautious care. Partly to insure his sovereigns' interest in another expedition, partly because he himself was dizzied by his achievement, he had let his expectations count as certainties; and now the Kings were counting certainties too. He had been proud of his titles, his prerogatives, his fleet of seventeen ships, sailing out of Cadiz: now, as he lay beneath his emblazoned coverlet, and thought of today's troubles and tomorrow's anxieties, how ardently he must have regretted the heavy burden he had assumed!

And the Court grew eager for the mirage to materialize. In August, 1495, Jaime Ferrer, jeweller to the Queen at Burgos, wrote by the Queen's order to "the most magnificent and honorable Sir, Admiral of the Indies, at the Great Island of Cibao." The letter stated that its humble author had made many travels in the Orient, had conversed with Hindoo, Arab and Ethiopian, and had learned that there was great store of gold and precious stones to be found in the torrid regions, in the countries inhabited by the black races. It hinted that the Queen wondered why her most faithful servant did not seek out these peoples, so that he might find the treasures of gold, of jewels, of aromatic spices and oils which they most certainly possessed . . .

On the eleventh of January, 1496, Christopher disembarked at Cadiz. He had come no nearer to the El Dorado than before, and he brought back no greater treasure. He had promised to seek out the gold of the Indies. What his reception would be, returning empty-handed, he well knew.

VIII.   THE PARADISE OF MAN

This time, he was kept a full month waiting before, at last, the Kings deigned to receive him. The Court lay then at Burgos, capital of Old Castille, and there was a marked difference in their greeting. Their doubts had been carefully fed by his enemies—doubts not only as to the value of his discovery but his own ability, even his honest desire, to exploit it. The Queen alone still gave him her confidence.

But his arrival had been on the heels of a magnificent festival, celebrating the double marriage of her son Don Juan and her daughter Doña Juana with the two children of the Emperor Maximilian; the expensive ceremony had been a heavy drain on her ebbing resources. Nevertheless, she found means, eventually, to outfit another flotilla for the west

Having obtained the necessary funds, however, this time did not completely clear him of his difficulties. He needed men, and the Spanish soldiers of fortune were not so eager to seek the Indies as before; their predecessors, those of the fifteen hundred, had put a tarnish on the El Dorado. "Those who had gone with the Admiral," wrote Fernandez de Oviedo, gentleman-in-waiting to the Infante, "came back so weakened, so chafed by disease and so ill-visaged that they seemed more like men dead than living: they so railed against the Indies, and the life there, that none was willing to go there afterward." And he adds, "Truly, even if the King had given me the Indies in my own right, I think I should never agree to go there, if I knew I should suffer as these men had suffered."

Christopher was forced, at last, to resort to the same means as had been employed at Palos, to recruit his crews. The Kings issued a proclamation, offering amnesty and privilege to all who would enroll. Those under the penalty of death were pardoned, on condition that they spend two years in the colonies; a year's enlistment sufficed for all lesser penalties, save with those condemned for heresy, treason or counterfeiting. Debtors were freed of their obligations. Men serving sentences at hard labor could have their sentences commuted, if they would serve with the Admiral. Even such inducements failed to hasten enlistment.

Meanwhile, tragedy had visited the Queen. Don Juan, her only son, had died. He died in his nineteenth year, on

the fourth of October, 1497 and at his burial the whole
nation went into mourning. Shops were closed and workmen left their benches for a period of forty days. The
Court wore black; the horses of the nobles were draped
with the mourning cloth. "Never was there a death," says
a contemporary chronicler, "which occasioned such deep
and general lamentation throughout the land."

In the height of the mourning, another blow fell. His
widow, Margaret of Austria, was delivered of a still-born
infant, a few months after pregnancy, and with this event
the hope of a male heir in the direct line of succession died
too. Isabella, unconsolable, gave over her nights to prayer
and weeping; by day, however, she forgot none of her
duties. A mark of her consideration for those about her
is seen in her treatment of Columbus. Both his sons, Fernando and Diego, had been pages to Don Juan; she saw
to it that both found places in her own entourage.

Some time earlier, a patent of the Kings had established
in Columbus' name a *mayorazgo*, or perpetual entail of
his estates. At the same time he had been offered the grant
of a large tract of land in Hispaniola, together with the
title of count or duke, as he preferred. Through prudence
or modesty, he had renounced these, preferring that "his
heirs shall never use any other signature than that of 'the
Admiral,' *el Almirante*, whatever other titles and honors
may belong to them." This was the name he had won by

193

his achievements, and it was an honest pride that made him wish by that name to be remembered.

He now prepared, by right of his *mayorazgo*, to invest his son Diego as heir of his title and estate. The document by which he formalized the act gives an insight into his state of mind at the time. More and more, it would seem, he was turning back his eyes toward the land of his birth—"Genoa, the noble city, and most powerful on the seas."

"I direct that my son Don Diego and those others who succeed him," he provides, "shall maintain at all times, in the city of Genoa, a person of our lineage, to establish his home and his family there; and shall provide him with a pension sufficient to support him honorably, as befits our position: and this because, being native and well-established in the city, he may when need comes the better obtain aid and encouragement from the Republic, since there it was that I had birth."

His heirs are directed to invest as much of their income as they may in the *Banca di San Giorgio*, making ready to aid the Kings in the conquest of Jerusalem or even, if necessary, to undertake its reduction at their own expense. He exhorts them always to support the Pope and the Church against the attacks of heretics, and to further the glory and the prosperity of Genoa. To his son he recommends the construction of a hospital at Española, and asks that masses be said there for his soul, and his forefathers', and his descendants'.

Throughout is apparent a concern—but a reasonable and honorable desire it is—that his name and his glory may be kept alive and resplendent—that name which by his own efforts he had raised from obscurity almost to the rank of kings, that glory which his own determination had achieved.

His family had become his chief preoccupation. Fernando, his son, tells us that Christopher never swore by any other symbol than "by Saint Ferdinand," his king's name. His patriotism had not secured his position from the affronts to which sudden exaltation is subject, and the bitterest of these came from families themselves a little uncertain in their pretensions, the *casas agraviados*—"enhanced families"—the parvenus of the day. The true aristocrats—the Excellencies of Castille, caballeros and hidalgos of ancient blood—all had their *casa solar*—the ancestral mansion or castle, with the arms and coronet to which they were entitled sculptured over the portal. Christopher's past lay in the *via del Mulcento*.

He never forgot it, nor was he allowed to; hatred from without intensified his inner instinct of affection toward his family. Long afterward he wrote to his son, "Ten brothers would not be too many for you. My surest friends have been my brothers." And so he called them to him, linking his fortunes with theirs. A notary's act remains, by which in 1496 his four cousins, all weavers, bound themselves to contribute equal shares toward the expenses of sending one of their number into Spain. Later, the cousin, Gianotto, or Giano-Antonio, had risen to the command of one of the Admiral's caravels. Like the Cossack to the saddle, these Genoese, whatever their professions, seemed born to the sea.

But if he favored those of his relatives who seemed capable of advancement, he was inexorable with those of them who had not in their natures to rise. So Bianchinetta, his sister, was left to the side-street society for which she was fitted, peddling cheese and neighborhood gossip with her husband Bavarello, in their little shop. His father, too, he had long ignored; even the memory of these unworthies was forgotten.

At the Spanish Court, it was of course impossible to deny the facts of his origin; he tried, however, to mitigate their humbleness by reference to a more illustrious, though imaginary, ancestry. It is strange that a man so brave before greater dangers should fear so simple an avowal as that of his own honest birth. He concealed it even from his children, leading them, like those around him, to believe that his family, though poor, had sprung from ancient and exalted sources, and that great captains were among his forebears.

But in this, of course, he was only following the spirit

196

of his age. In a society where rank and lineage were its first observances, to avow his humble birth would have utterly discredited him. In addition, Spain more than any other nation, was passing through a period of social upset which followed naturally after her long wars. The older chivalry had disappeared; new families rose to replace those that had declined, building themselves each an ancestry to suit their present exaltation.

Columbus, however, had risen faster and higher than any other. His miraculous metamorphosis from penniless outlander to High Admiral of half the world could not but provoke envy and hatred among the less fortunate climbers. The smaller fry were forced to content themselves with slander and back-biting. But there were other, more powerful personages whose ill-will could be more dangerous.

So now the members of the Indian Ministry met him with the same passive, stubborn resistance which the citizenry of Palos had offered him before. His requests were ignored and disregarded; when backed by the Queen's command, they were more courteously received, but just as slow of execution. At the head of the Ministry was Don Juan de Fonseca. Christopher, in despair, set himself deliberately to conciliate this personage.

It was, from the start, a hopeless task. The two men were born to be at odds. Fonseca, to his very marrow, was a bureaucrat. In private life, he numbered eight hundred

COLUMBUS LANDING IN AMERICA.

FROM DE BRY'S "VOYAGES."

"The Admiral erected a cross of wood, ordered trumpets to sound, and proclaimed to all who might hear, the degree of the sovereigns he represented, and their peaceful intention."

slaves among his dependants. In public life as well, in the various state departments he had administered, he had grown to regard his clerks and underlings much as he did his slaves at home. A pedant, a Tory, a stickler for tradition and a stand-patter in routine, he visioned the newly discovered colonies only as fresh material for his ledger-books, and fashioned their policies to conform to the dry exactitude of the counting-room. To such a man, the point of view—even the very existence—of Columbus could never be other than an obstacle to his doctrine.

In spite of all, however, and with great aid from the Queen, Christopher at last made ready for the third adventure. On May 30, 1498, he lighted seventeen silver lamps before the altar in the Church of Our Lady of Charity in the town of San Lucar. From the same port, on the same day, his fleet of six caravels headed into the west. Steering more southerly than before, on the first of August —having, some days earlier, touched at an island which he christened *Isla de Gracia*—Island of Mercy—he discovered the continent of South America, landing near the Bay of Paria.

The sailors sang the *Salve Regina*; the notaries drew up the formal documents by which the Catholic Rulers took possession of the land; the Admiral erected a cross of wood, ordered trumpets to sound, and proclaimed to all who might hear, the degree of the sovereigns he represented and their peaceful intention. He then wrote to the Kings, including a chart of his voyage and a few pearls he had obtained from the natives, and informed them that at last his prayers had been realized: he had found the western continent!

And there was more. A short distance away, they discovered the river called the Oronoco. The great flood rolled down through the jungle, its waters warm and fragrant, its current sweeping far out into the ocean. And Christopher recalled how in the Old Testament there is a description of a mighty river which irrigates the Oriental countries and has its source in Eden, the Paradise of Man. Might not this enormous stream be the spring of all rivers as the Bible mentioned? His mind, as we have seen, had been turning more and more toward the mysteries of religion. Now, he asked himself, might not the tales of El Dorado have been but halting descriptions of the golden birthplace of man? Following this river to its sources, would he not find, not only Cypangu, but Paradise as well?

For the moment, however, there were other, though more earthly, matters to occupy him. He remembered the fate of the first garrison at Navidad; now he was anxious to learn how his brother, and the second company, had fared. He sailed, accordingly, for Española. On the way, his journal records, a violent attack of gout, followed by a painful affection of the eyes, recalled again to him, as by an

200

omen, the frailty of humankind and the mystic power of the Faith. Meanwhile, as he neared the settlement, the gravest fears beset him. He had left the suburbs of Paradise; he was approaching a kind of human hell.

On his departure for Spain, two years before, Christopher had left a Castillian, Francisco Roldan, as *Alcalde*— that is, Chief Magistrate. Before a year had passed, this functionary was leading a rebellion against his nominal chief, Bartholomew Columbus, left as Lieutenant-Governor of the colony. Bartholomew was a man of tremendous physical—but weaker moral—force. He had not been able to quell the revolt. Christopher arrived to find the whole establishment in the grip of civil war.

Matters had gone too far for force. He tried persuasion. The temper of rebellion would not be swayed. He offered safe-conduct home to Roldan and all his party—including their slaves, their native wives, if they wished, and the children they had borne. The men refused to go. In the end, the Admiral capitulated. Roldan and the rebels received a general pardon, and were reinstated in their offices.

Barely had this been accomplished, before a fleet of four caravels sailed into the harbor of Española. Their commander was Alonso de Hojeda, who had distinguished himself in the native rebellion by the capture of the *cacique* Caonabo—"The Master of the Golden House."

201

The colonial trade, it will be remembered, belonged by right to the Crown. Upon such commerce, under the terms of the Capitulation of Santa Fe, Christopher was entitled to levy a certain share of profit.

At first, the terms of this agreement were strictly observed, so that even the Duke of Medina-Cœli, who had, by the aid he had given Columbus, a certain claim to consideration, was refused by the Queen when he solicited permission to send out a fleet of ships to trade with the colonies.

With time, however, the monopoly grew weaker in its enforcement. The Kings, as they sometimes do, forgot their solemn "Capitulation." In 1495, Fonseca perceived in this condition an opportunity to weaken further the power of the Admiral. At his suggestion, trade with the new world was declared open and free from restriction by the Crown, save that they must register at Cadiz, under the control of the Indian Ministry. Thus adroitly, Christopher, hardly knowing, was deprived of all share in the profits of his discovery, and their supervision made over to his enemy.

Hojeda had been a page in the household of the Duke of Medina-Cœli. He now commanded the first attempt to take advantage of the new situation. With the fleet came the Florentine, Amerigo Vespucci, later to be known in his own right as an explorer. At the time, his importance lay in the fact that he was a partner with the famous devices by which men were made to tell their secrets. By comparison with such as these, the Indians began to regret the Carib cannibals, and revise the demonology of their religions.

So, in disorder, rebellion and brutality, the islands which seven years earlier had been "a paradise to look upon" grew rank and stagnant, and Christopher's authority diminished day by day. Fonseca and his following were not ignorant of the condition. So far, however, though they withheld all aid from Columbus, they dared not openly side with the rebellion.

Moreover, it must be admitted that Columbus was primarily unfitted for such a post as that he held. A commander, he was no organizer; a persuader, he knew nothing of intrigue, nor the cautious middle courses by which intrigue may be checked. He was a dreamer—and increasingly so, now that the mystic side of him overcame the adventurer—and such men are always baffled by the petty motives of men. So on the one hand, his followers threatened and blustered, exasperated by slow pay, scant rations and the decline of their hopes; on the other, the Court, the King and all about him were slowly being alienated by the slander and hatred which he was powerless to combat.

Though he was impotent against difficulties which one more adroit might have surmounted, Christopher was not insensible to them. The letter which he sent back to the

THE ORIGIN OF THE EGG-TRICK LEGEND.

FROM DE BRY'S "VOYAGES."

. . . " . . . seated at a great feast with many of the Spanish nobility, the conference turned upon India; and one of those present said to him: 'Even if you had not found the Indies, there were not wanting those in this Spain of ours, who would have attempted the same thing; for Spain abounds in great and ingenious men'. Columbus made no reply; however, he ordered an egg to be placed upon the table, and requested all present to try if they could make it stand on end. . . . When none succeeded, he showed how it could be done."

Kings, in report of his voyage, reveals his apprehension and his pathetic bafflement.

"May God forgive," he writes, "those persons who have opposed and still do oppose an undertaking so excellent as this, hindering and preventing it from its consummation, with no thought for the glory and grandeur which its success might command for Your Majesties, throughout the Universe. They have no thought for anything but for lies: asserting that so much has been spent on the voyages and that as yet no ships have come back loaded with gold, they forget how short a time we have been searching, and how many obstacles we have met with; they forget too that no other Sovereign in Spain has ever acquired lands outside his own domain, except Your Majesties, who have won another world to themselves, where our Holy Faith may be propagated, and whence great profit may be drawn; and although so far no ship's full of gold have been seen, we have discovered enough of the metal, and enough other precious things, and sent them back for samples, to prove that if only sufficient time be given us, the profit will be great indeed."

He adds that the *Adelantado*, Bartholomew, is setting forth with three ships to explore the newly discovered continent, "where I am convinced in my soul is to be found the Paradise of Man."

And now one of his abilities to which he owed much

of his success was turning toward his undoing. That eloquence of his, the persuasive charm in narrative and argument which had established him in the graces of the Court and won him his ambition, was now almost beyond control. Confounding in his mind the deductions of the cosmographer with the speculations of the mystic—led on, too, in his anxiety to combat his enemies, he was expounding theories which even in that day seemed fantastic. This new will-of-the-wisp of his—this Eden unattained he now professed to discover—one can imagine the advantage his enemies drew from so naïve an assertion. "And if so in this case," they argued, "why not with the rest? Are not these treasures which, year after year, he claims always to have within reach of his finger-tips—are not these, too, chimeras like his Paradise?"

No wonder Christopher, sensing this, was uneasy and restless, begging again and again that the Kings will proclaim their confidence in him. "Let water fall drop by drop on the hard stone long enough," he wrote, "and it will wear it away in the end."

So slow, but so relentless, had been the work of his enemies, and the rock of his reputation was nearly worn away. His life, so far, had held nine years of preparation, poverty and delay; eight years of transcendent glory had followed them. The years of bitterness and disgrace were now to come.

208

IX. THE EAGLE CHAINED

Spain gave us Calderon and Goya. Spain gave us Don Quixote, and before that the whole fabric of chivalry which Cervantes destroyed. Spain gave us mantillas, sherry wine, castanets, the vogue for gypsy dances—and romance. She gave us the mercenary soldier; she taught us the power of light cavalry, and the might of disciplined infantrymen. Paradoxically, too, she gave us something else which fits oddly with this picture of plumes and lace and bravado. She gave us the bureaucrat, the despotism of routine.

Perhaps it was one of the Moorish influences in her society, for the Moors had an awed deference for the written word. Perhaps it was an off-shoot of the stubborn civic constitution of her people, who clung grimly to even the most unimportant privilege, until their jurisprudence was an inextricable tangle of custom and observance. However it was, it is certain that the hardy knights of Castille, if they bent before no other foe, bowed low to the authority of the bureaucrat. Behind all the turbulence of her feudatories, all the prance and glamor of her knights, is seen the dull, methodical, inflexible power of the book-keeper and the pedant. Here, if nowhere else, the pen was mightier than the sword, and the pen to the last represented tradition, ancient usage and routine.

Thus, in the end, the glory that her blue blood had won for her was drowned in the black of ink and the wheels of conquest stalled in the dust of the accounting-room, but not before the Crown of Spain had passed into Austria, bringing with it the habit of the ledger, the secretarial re-port, and all the traditional red-tape now part of every government.

Meanwhile, these spectacled hidalgos, opposed by in-stinct to all the broad daring of the adventurer, bent their energies to circumvent the plans of Christopher, most ad-venturous of them all.

For the moment, the favor in which the Queen held him was their chief obstacle. It was to counteract this that a charge was advanced against him which is still often men-tioned to his disfavor, although in respect to it he was precisely no more innocent and no more guilty than any other man of his age. The charge was that he was engaged in the slave trade. When even native Spaniards were born to feudal servitude; when Moors, Arabs and African Ne-groes were dumped in cargoes at every port and sold on the market-block; when no objection of any importance to the whole theory of slavery had found its way into the philosophy of any nation; it would have been almost a miracle if Christopher had felt toward the traffic in any way other than he did.

Moreover, even if he had been so advanced a humanitarian as to wish to prevent it, it is extremely doubtful if he could have done so. We have seen the futility of his resistance to Hojeda; we have seen how powerless he was to dominate his own colonists. In default of gold, the slave trade offered one of the most profitable means to exploit the colonies. That he permitted the traffic to continue is evidence only of the character of his day; if he had tried to stop it, the general outcry would certainly have been great enough to ruin him.

Nevertheless, some small outcry was raised among the malcontents. It is odd indeed that it should have come from Fonseca, himself the proprietor of eight hundred slaves, but no one thought of that. And in the telling, of course, the tale lost nothing of its spice. It would seem that, far from merely indulging in the traffic, Christopher was making it his chief source of wealth; and not only were shiploads being sent to Spain, but in the colonies themselves, the colonists, led on by the Admiral, had hundreds of natives at their bidding, and whole haremsful of the native women.

The Queen was touched both in her piety and in her pride. "By what right," she exclaimed, "does the Admiral deem himself privileged to dispose of my vassals, to his own profit?"

Meanwhile, the gold of the Indies remained elusive; the little sent back was always far less than had been expected. And, meanwhile, the clamor grew, from colonists and adventurers, returned minus illusions and pay. Crowds besieged the Court, begging, pleading, commanding. Rancorous against the Admiral, many would vent their rage on his sons.

"Look at them!" they would cry, "Little gutter-snipes! Sons of this Admiral from no one knows where, who doesn't know where he's going either! Listen, you two: has your high-and-mighty father ever told you where he expects to find this dreamland he's looking for? Do you know how many honest Spanish gentlemen he's led to their deaths, hunting for it?"

Diego and Fernando, though pages to the Queen, had many a bitter moment, in the Queen's palace.

In Granada, when the Kings passed through the square at the Alhambra, their escort had to clear the way for them, while crowds assailed them from the marble steps on either side. Ragged, weather-beaten, blear-eyed, chewing wild grapes and holding out the clusters for the Sovereigns to see: "Look at the misery the Admiral has brought us to!" they cried. "Give us our pay! Give us the money due us!"

The general fever of complaint in the end had its effect. The Queen was a woman of deliberate mind and honest purpose. She had trusted Christopher, and was willing to trust him further. But if all the world hated the man, there must be some reason for it. She decided to send a commission of inquiry to Española. Once more the slippered, secretarial gentry sharpened their quill-pens and ruffled their reams of paper.

There were whisperings in the antechambers, conferences in the counting-rooms. The officers of the Ministry, for the most part, had already solved the problem to their own satisfaction. *One*: There was gold in the Indies. *Two*: Columbus had discovered the Indies. Logically, then, it followed that Columbus had the gold. To force him to reveal it, therefor, would not only avenge them and their caste against the upstart, but enrich the Queen and them, as well. When at last Francisco de Bobadilla was chosen to head the commission, Columbus had already been tried and convicted in their minds.

There is a curious twist of interest in his appointment. Beatriz de Bobadilla had been one of Christopher's earliest friends, had favored him and believed in him when he had first arrived, still dusty from the road, and penniless, at Seville. And Beatriz was nearly related to the newly chosen judge and commissioner, Francisco. He held at the Court the rank of *criado*—a sort of gentleman-in-waiting to the royal family. He was poor, but a knight of the Order of Calatrava, and thoroughly imbued with the pride of his caste. It was natural that he should detest the parvenu Columbus, and envy him for his attainments. But it is probable, too, that his venom now was increased by the very fact of the favors Beatriz had shown his enemy in the earlier days. Powerless then to interfere, the opportunity to do so now seemed doubly desirable.

So he sailed, his judgment already in his mind, and determined to waste no time with courtesies or judicial amenities, to reach his ends. An order in judgement, signed by the Kings and left blank for his decision, gave him full powers to act.

He arrived early in the autumn of 1500. Christopher and Bartholomew were away on a trip of inspection about the island. As the vessel bearing the Commissioner came into the port of Santo Domingo, he noticed the bodies of seven men hanging on the gallows of the town. In those days there was nothing unusual in that. Hangings were frequent, and the bodies were left to rot in the chains, to advertise the penalties of crime. But the victims here were Spaniards, like Bobadilla himself, and the man who had commanded their death was a foreigner. Without more ado, the Commissioner seized the government, assumed the post of Vice-Regent, confiscated all of Christopher's belongings, and occupied his home.

Warned of this, Columbus hastened to return. Bobadilla refused to receive him, threw him into prison without a hearing. Bartholomew prepared to resist the order, but Christopher counselled him to submit, for the Kings' authority was vested in this man. The *Adelantado* was imprisoned immediately.

The arrest was sudden; the trial was slow. For a time, those who had rebelled against the Admiral gave way to a kind of holiday, to celebrate his downfall. Functionaries of the government, colonists, gold-hunters—all gathered to release their pent-up hate, now that he was defenseless. They called him thief and muddle-wit. *"Fallador! Fantastico!"* they yelled at him in his chains. Monks of the Franciscan Order broke a spiteful silence, wrote to Cardinal Cisneros, inveighing against him, calling him "like a Pharaoh," for his heathenish doctrine, for his gold.

After the shock and anger of the sudden moment, Columbus turned inward to his mysticism for consolation. He lay in his prison cell and thought of Job, and the dark mystery of the will of God. He thought how he had been chosen among all men to lead the way out and across the ocean to the new continent. He thought how, afterward, his days had been full of glory and pomp and grandiloquence. And now the passion had come; uplifted above all other men before, he was now to be cast down, so low as to be beneath the lowliest, so that all might see the tinsel that was power, the sham that was the favor of princes.

He lay in his cell for two months. During that time, Bobadilla had been about the business of his trial. Under the conditions, it was hardly more than a burlesque. All the colonists, all the horde of the greedy, the get-rich-quick were against the fallen Admiral. His sailors, the men of his ships who had sailed under him, alone stood out for him. But their voice was lost among the others. In the end, Bobadilla handed down his decision.

The Admiral was to be sent home to Spain. He .was to be embarked on the *Gorda*, which was to sail at once. Extreme care must be taken that he be kept strictly confined and in chains during the voyage—as Fernando Columbus observes in the *Historie*, "lest he might by chance escape, and swim back to the island."

So, close-guarded, he was brought to the caravel. Here the fidelity of the only men who understood his nature was made touchingly evident. Ordered to rivet the chains about his hands and ankles, the sailors, to a man, refused. For a moment there was hesitation, then a cook, by name Espinosa, stepped forward and rivetted the irons in place. Immediately anchor was weighed and the ship sailed. Out of sight of land, the captain Alonso de Vallejo courteously offered to strike off the chains and give Christopher the freedom of the ship. Columbus refused. "Let it be as it has been ordered," he said.

What were his thoughts in the long days at sea, no one can know. Before, he had walked the deck, scanned the horizon, watched the sails, commanding the helm to be put down this way or that, ordering his men about their duties as the ship drove on. Now, he lay below, while another captain held the ship to the ocean track that he himself had discovered. It stormed, and he heard the surge and crash of the waves against the sides and the hurried steps of the crew overhead. The wind died and they lay wallowing; the damp got into his bones.

He was a dreamer, but still no child in the ways of the world. He had known poverty, distrust, deceit; he had seen the ruin that men's spite may cause. So now, as they neared home, he grew calmer. He had faith in Isabella; or rather he knew that her faith in him was such that, if he could only obtain audience with her, if he could only make her understand the factions and resentments that had opposed him, he knew she would understand. He must be eloquent, crafty and adroit with the others; with the Queen he knew he need only be sincere.

The days passed. At last he heard the rattling roar and splash as they let go the anchor. They were in port at last, in Cadiz harbor. Spain, where now Fonseca and his enemies awaited him!

But the voyage had given him time to make his plans. Immediately, he found means to forward a letter to his friend, Doña Juana de Torre, formerly governess to the dead Infante, and always the great favorite of Isabella.

"Most kind and virtuous lady," he wrote, "although now for the first time you hear me complain against the world, it is not but that it has been the world's way to treat me ill: it has visited a thousand affronts on me, and I have resisted them all, until now the moment comes when neither courage nor good conduct can help me; I am cruelly borne down. Hope in the God who created us all alone remains to me: always in the past He has sustained me. Once before, and not long ago, I was cast down even more low than now, but He came, raising me with his divine strength, and saying: 'O man of little faith, arise; it is I; be without fear' . . . I came to the service of the Kings, giving them greater marks of my fidelity than any other man; I have done for them more than any other prince has had from a subject . . . God made me his messenger toward the new skies and lands of which He spoke in the Apocalypse through the mouth of Saint John and that of Isaiah, and He showed the way by which I might discover them. All were incredulous, save the Queen, whose servant I am; to her God gave the spirit of intelligence, and the courage necessary, and endowed her with the grant of the new world as to His best-loved daughter. I sought to take possession of the territory in the royal name; all the rest, seeking to conceal the depth of their ignorance, were busy telling of the dangers of the journey, and its expense. But her Majesty fostered it in spite of them all, and aided it with all she could give.

"Seven years passed in conferences, and nine more in the execution of undertakings which are remarkable enough to remain forever in the memories of mankind: but now no consideration is shown me on that account . . . Now I am in such condition that even the vilest may affront me; but, God willing, the day will come when none can hear of my suffering without regret. If I had stolen away the Indies and made them over to the Moors, I could not be held by the Spaniards in greater enmity."

And then he recounted the events at Española, after the arrival of Bobadilla:

"Rightfully, I should be judged in the capacity of a captain, sent out from Spain to conquer a numerous and warlike nation, whose religions and customs are completely contrary to our own, whose inhabitants live remote in the mountains, without regular domicile either for them or for us, and where, by the grace of God, I have succeeded in bringing a whole new world under the rule of the King and the Queen, our Masters; and by virtue of which, Spain, called until then poor among nations, is now the richest of all . . . I should be judged as a captain who has borne arms for years ceaselessly, never once laying them aside . . . I should be judged by knights of adventure, by men of arms and not of the pen, unless they be Greek or Roman, or some one of these moderns of whom there are in Spain so many, for still more have I been injured by this: that in the Indies there exists neither right nor justice, nor are any treaties recognized.

"Already the way is open to the gold and pearls we sought; it is certain that precious stones, spices and a thousand other goods of value will be found. Please Heaven that, as surely as no greater harm becomes me than I have already suffered, so surely will I undertake, in the name of Our Lord, my first voyage on the undertaking which, in the letter sent by me in charge of Antonio de Torre, I described to Their Majesties, toward Araby into Mecca, which I suggested after the partition of the sea and land between Spain and Portugal; and that thereafter will I go up toward the Arctic Pole, as I wrote and described in a letter to the Monastery of La Mejorada. And as to the certainty of gold, this is by the assurance of Our Lord, who came to me on the day of his Nativity, as I lay tormented and afflicted as much by the wickedness of my Christians as by my natives, and so despairing that I had thought I must flee to save my life; he came, soothing me miraculously, and saying: 'Take courage, do not give up to sadness and fear; I will look to all; the seven years of the search for gold are not yet past, and in this as in all other things I will give you your wishes.' "

And again, he repeats the misdeeds of Bobadilla, pointing out his injustice, and concluding with a cry almost of defiance to his Sovereigns:

"May God, the Supreme Master, make use of his power and his all-knowledge as in the past, and punish the ungrateful!"

The excess of malice displayed by Bobadilla acted, as it turned out, to defeat itself. The spectacle of the Admiral cast without trial into prison and sent home in chains was enough to touch even the hardest heart. The Kings commanded him to be liberated immediately. Court held at Granada, the ancient capital of the Moors, called by them Hisnal-Romman—Palace of the Pomegranates. Christopher arrived there on December seventeenth, and was received with great courtesy and marks of signal favor.

The instinct of the desert, where water is a greater boon than diamonds, had not been dead in the Moors when they built the Alhambra. The lace of its architecture is everywhere reflected in pools among the gardens; fountains tinkle everywhere, great vases stand at the sides of every entrance door, full of flowing water, and in the famous Court of the Lions the air is rippling with the splashing jets of water.

Here, then, the glory of Spain gave color to the majesty

THE 'TABULA NOVARUM INSULARUM.'

FROM THE COSMOGRAPHIA OF MUNSTER.

It shows the coast of Paria, "abundant in gold"; the land of cannibals; "Zipangri," or Cypangu—the Island of Gold; and the seven thousand four hundred and forty-eight islands of the Indies.

INDIA superior

Cathay
Quinfay

Calenfuin

Inf. pidonum

Inf. infortunate

Archipelagus 7448 insularū

Zipangri

Chamaho

Panuco

Inf. ſ. Tornarū

Terra florida

Canigra

Nouus orbis

Inſula Atlantica quam vocant Braſilij & Americam.

CVBA

Iaina

Iſpana

Iſabella

Borica

Berfije

PARIAS ſaluandır auro & margaritis

Iamica

FRANCISCA

C. Britonum

Oceanus occidentalis

Exteriores

Die Nüw Welt
Regio Gigantum

7. infulæ Martguenara

Caribali

Dominica

S. Iacobi

Antilia

Saua

Inf. Helperidum

Fortunatæ inf.

Medera

AFRICÆ pars

Hiſpania

Sinus Atlantiens

FRANCISI

of the Moors, and here the Kings received their servant, Columbus. But all their welcome seemed a little empty to him; the bitterness of his treatment still rankled in his heart. Pleasant words had been spoken. No mention of reparation, no offer that would assure his future had been made. He remained still but half cleared of his disgrace. Angelo Trevisan, secretary to the Venetian Legation at the Court, wrote in August, 1501, to Admiral Domenico Malipiero, "Columbus' situation is now most unfavorable; he has very little money, and is regarded with disfavor by the Sovereigns."

Christopher himself, under the sting of his misfortunes, withdrew deeper and deeper into mysticism. He read the Bible, searched as well as with his limited education he might the classics, finding confirmation everywhere of the divine nature of his mission. Going further, he found passages in Scripture which prophesy his discoveries, and forecast the deliverance of Jerusalem which he was bent on accomplishing. Writing sometimes in Latin, sometimes in Castillian, he compiled all these evidences, sending them to a monk of the Chartreuse Order, Father Gaspar Gorrido. This "Prophetical Book"[1] he intended to address to the

---

[1] Incipit liber sive manipulus de auctoritatibus, dictis, ac sententus, et prophetus circa materiam recuperande sancte civitatis, et montis Dei Syon, ac inventionis et conversionis insularum Indie, et omnium gentium atque nationum, ad Ferdinandum et Helysabeth, etc., reges nostros hyspanos. (Here begins the book

Kings, and to the Pope. The year following, he wrote to the Pontiff, Alexander VI, enumerating his discoveries, which he said included fourteen hundred islands, three hundred thirty-three leagues in the continent of Asia, as well as Tarsis, Ophir and Cypangu. He revealed that, from the very first voyage he had undertaken, he had been accustomed to keep a journal, drawn up after the manner of Caesar's Commentaries. To the Venetian Ambassador he promised copies of all the letters he had written to the Kings, during his journeys. He delved in the ancient authors, annotating the "Lives of Plutarch," which had been translated in Spanish by Alonzo de Palencia, and published at Seville in 1491. He quoted Seneca as an authority, citing in his "Prophetical Book" a passage from Medea, which he claimed clearly foretold his adventure:

"At a time far distant in the future, a day shall come when the Ocean will release its bondage, and a great continent will be opened, and a new sea-sailor, like that Tiphis who piloted Jason, will discover a new world."

Curiously, too—but whether intentionally or unconsciously,—the text he quotes had been altered. Seneca speaks only of the Ocean, mentioning no mariner. Colum-

or manual of the sources, sayings, omens and prophesies concerning the recovery of the Holy City and the Mount of Zion, as well as the discovery and conversion of the Indian Islands, and all their peoples and nations, to the dominion of Ferdinand and Isabella, our Spanish Kings.)

bus, to speak truly, was more at ease with his convictions at the helm of a ship, than in the library. Oviedo calls him "learned in Latin," but it is probable that his compositions in that language were revised by some scholarly monk of his acquaintance. In Castillian, however, he was completely at home, and his style had become so thoroughly a part of him that in it one clearly sees the imprint of his character, his virtues and his weaknesses.

At times he affects a spurious classicism, straining to imitate the stylists of the day. But when he forgets affectation, and speaks out from the honesty of his heart; when he abandons the veiled voice of the courtier and adopts the tone of the man who has out-shouted tempests, then one sees him as he was, the deep-browed, red-cheeked, white-haired veteran of the seas, with a mystic ecstasy in his eyes, and in his mouth the moving phrases of a modern Job.

In spite of his age, his gout, and the infirmities that had followed on his stormy life, Christopher still felt himself predestined to greater and more glorious accomplishments; in this relation, his literary activities and his runic reading served as a balm to his present misfortunes and a stimulant toward future attainment. His great obsession was to reach the lands of spice and treasure; once discovered, he would use their profits to finance the recapture of the Holy Land from the infidel. Born to the sea, the life ashore was a burden to him. He had, moreover, another reason to hasten the attainment of his aims. He had now arrived at the conviction—based on his reading of the "Prophetical Book"—that the earth itself was doomed to an early destruction. Its life, he was assured, would not continue more than one hundred and fifty years longer!

IX. AT SEA AGAIN

T HE functionaries of the Indian Ministry, however, had no fears on the subject of the destruction of the earth. And the Kings, in spite of the proof advanced by their Admiral as to his divine mission, showed little disposition to reinstate him as their Vice-Regent in the Indies. Instead, they appointed Don Nicolas de Ovando to that position. But if, in their opinion, Columbus had shown himself an uninspired executive, they still retained their faith in him as a mariner, and in this capacity believed they could still find use for his courage and experience. As for his dreams of world-dominion and religious conquest, they were inclined to view them a little cynically: did he not claim to have discovered the Indies, and found the entrance to the Paradise of Man, while everyone knew he had merely stumbled on a group of barbarous islands, poor in wealth and inhabited by savages?

And so Don Nicolas de Ovando sailed away to undertake the duties of his high post, with a fleet of twenty-five great ships for convoy. Christopher, meanwhile, was given three battered caravels and a tiny sailing ship with which to prosecute his further exploration. There was, however, no lack of pleasant speeches.

"Be assured," the Kings wrote him on March 14, 1502, "that We were most deeply grieved to learn of your imprisonment, as We have shown you by every token, and all the world besides; and this is proved by the fact that, as soon as we learned of what had been done you, we hastened to make amends, and you know well the good opinion in which We have ever held you, and now We are pleased to do all things possible to the end that you will be honored and obeyed."

In the instructions which accompanied this letter, Christopher was ordered to take along with him on his voyage an interpreter in the Arab tongue; at the same time, he was authorized to bring his younger son Fernando with him. The Sovereigns' first concern, naturally, was to gain a monopoly over the commerce and resources of all the islands their Admiral might discover. To this end, he was instructed to prepare a memorandum, attested by the royal notary, setting forth their products and manufactures; the notary was installed, pro. tem., as a sort of supervisor of this commerce, with control over all goods imported or exported. By these means, it was hoped to reduce to a

228

minimum the delay, between discovery and exploitation.

Before he sailed, Christopher prepared another *mayor-azgo*, or entail, on his estate, and registered it before a notary. Among other items, he ordered Diego his son to pay one-tenth of his revenues to the city of Genoa, in order to reduce the tax on wheat and wine. At the same time he wrote to the Banca di San Giorgia, informing them of this decision.

Beside his interest in the welfare of his native town, Christopher's chief concern was to insure the preservation of his fame, and the appurtenances of his rank. Accordingly, he commanded a notary of Seville to draw up several copies of the letters-patent confirming his privileges. The original decrees he gave for safe-keeping to the monk, Father Gorricio; two copies were sent to the learned Nicolo de Oderigo, at one time Genoese Ambassador to Spain, now retired to Genoa.

But if, on the one hand, we see the man so enamored of his titles, so dazzled by the mere gilding of rank and privilege about his name that even in his life's crisis his first thought is to cling to them and insure their preservation, we must, on the other hand, admit that in practice he insisted on none of the pomp and extravagance that might have been his rank's observance. He lived simply, even with austerity. While all the court went richly embroidered and accoutered, in silks and satins, he was seen always in

229

the same rough garb, a kind of cowled, long-skirted frock, like a monk's robe, which he wore belted with the rope girdle of the Franciscans.

In this, of course, there may have been a kind of affectation, for sometimes a man's station seems more exalted, if he dress beneath it. But it seems probable there were other motives at work here. For Christopher was convinced that there was a divine purpose impelling him toward a divine fulfillment. Like a monk on a pilgrimage, he seized gratefully, even greedily, on all that might augment his power and insure his success, but in the prosecution of his mission he lived austere and humble.

On May 25, 1502, this Admiral of monkish manner boarded his flagship in Cadiz harbor and the little flotilla weighed for the open sea. He might discover what he might, sail where he would, with one exception—he was forbidden to touch at Española. Yet by the ironic fortune of the sea, it was here that he made the landfall. The sea was high; his flagship leaked and was in perilous condition; experienced navigator that he was, he read in every sign a portent of storm. Nevertheless, in this condition, Bobadilla refused to abate one jot of his power. Iron in his enmity to the last, he refused to permit his fallen rival to enter harbor. "Who is there, even Job himself," wrote Christopher, "who would not be near dead of despair, since now, and even when it means safety for myself, for my son, my brother and my friends, they forbid me to land and seek shelter in the very port which, by the effort of my blood and by the grace of God, I myself discovered for the glory of Spain?"

Then riding in the harbor was the fleet of Ovando, twenty-eight great ships. Don Nicolas had arrived; Bobadilla was preparing to lead the flotilla back to Spain again, with a load of the island produce. Even in his extremity, Christopher, hovering outside the harbor gates, found time to send a communication to his enemy, advising against departure. Bobadilla, as haughty as before, refused to accept his counsel.

And then befell one of those climactic and dramatic justifications which nature alone can sometimes develop. Scarcely had the Spanish fleet left its moorings before one of those tremendous hurricanes which strike like lightning in the tropics, came down on them. The great galleons were overwhelmed. Of them all, not more than three or four escaped. The flagship, with Bobadilla, Roldan and many other of the Admiral's enemies, was sunk and all on board were drowned. With them was lost its cargo, comprising two hundred thousand *castellanos* of gold. Columbus, more wise in the sea's ways, had sought shelter under the lee of the island, and rode the storm out in safety.

So, almost before his eyes, his strongest adversaries, together with the profits of their enterprise, were destroyed.

231

Columbus saw in it a portent of divine justification of his purpose. His opponents, staggered by the suddenness of the tragedy, accused him of black magic.

Christopher's purpose now was to discover a passage into the Indian Ocean. Though they seem ridiculous now, in the light of his information his conclusions were logical enough; he was convinced that there must be a strait somewhere between Cuba and the coast of Paria, by which he might enter the Asiatic waters. He set sail for the west.

On December 13, 1502, a cyclone came down on them. It was the first time he or any of his sailors had seen this terrifying phenomenon; they were thrown into the wildest confusion. Since his nautical experience failed him, Christopher had resource to religion. Consecrated candles were lighted at all the port-holes. The Admiral, donning the Franciscan girdle, recited the Gospel of Saint John; then, standing on the howling deck while the crew prayed, he cut the storm with strokes of his sword. The cyclone abated.

On Twelfth Night, after a long series of perils, they made the coast of the continent. The region was called by its natives Veragua. From them Columbus learned—or so he interpreted their jargon—that a rich and properous nation lived not far away, at a distance no greater than that between Pisa and Venice. Ten days farther on, lay the Ganges.

Christopher was anxious to continue. Already, from the

heights, he could smell a salty flavor in the western breeze
—the breeze from the Pacific. He was outvoted. Just beyond the horizon lay Mexico, with all the wealth and
treasure which Cortez, two decades later, was to uncover.
But Columbus' men refused to go on. In Veragua they
had found some few deposits of gold—small in yield and
difficult of working, but still gold. Moreover, the conviction had come to them that this, at last, was the fabled land
of Chersonesus, King Solomon's treasure-chest. So once
more Columbus' dream was thwarted; they remained at
Veragua, grubbing for a few nuggets of gold, while just
beyond them waited the justification of his ambitions, the
vindication of his dreams and the contradiction of his
enemies, in the crowded treasure-houses of the Aztec kings.

One night, after a day of storm and tropic heat, the
Admiral had a vision; in the darkness he heard a heavenly
voice, crying, "Oh! thoughtless one, slow and incredulous in the service of the Lord who reigns over all mankind! What more than for you did He do in the aid even
of Moses, or of David, his servant? From the day of
birth has He not watched over you, and when you came
to the time marked for you in your destiny, did He not
make your name remarkable throughout all the earth?
Did He not put the Indies into your hands, to dispose of
as you would? You had from Him the keys to the gates
of the Ocean, until then closed as by strong chains against

Man's access. By His work, your command is powerful across the breadth of great nations, and by His grace your glory is strong among the Christians. What greater favor than this did He show even to the people of Israel, when He led them out of Egypt? Or to David, the shepherd, whom He raised to the throne of Judea?

"Come, then, to the Lord, and depart from the way of error; His mercy is infinite. Your age will not prevent you from achievement; the Lord still holds in His hands a brilliant heritage for you. Was not Abraham well past his hundredth year when he gave birth to Isaac? And was Sarah much younger?

"You complain of the uncertainty of your fortunes: but speak now, is it the Lord or the world of man that has been unfaithful to you? For the Lord never takes back what He has given; He never betrays the faith He accords you. The work in His service once accomplished, He never pretends that it was not done according to His intention, or that by another way it might have been bettered. Never, to give proof of His power, does He make the weak suffer; His word is inviolable; all that He promises He performs, in even greater measure than need be: such is His way.

"Look, then, and see what the Lord has done for you, and what He does for all. Show you, therefor, the recompense you have had of Him, for the perils and dangers you have undergone in the service of others. Take confidence,

234

and fear not: all that you suffer is written as in marble, its memory will endure. His will is behind all."

The vision, however, did not signify the end of his difficulties. Disappointed and disgruntled, the little flotilla— now reduced to two caravels—left Veragua at last and coasted along the Honduras shore, then up the southern side of Cuba. Continuing north beyond the island's tip, they would have had Florida and the continent of North America almost within hail. But again, through his men's unwillingness, he was doomed to be halted, one step from the threshold of discovery.

Food was low. The men were wearied and weakened by their work in the mines at Veragua and the fevers that had followed; they were discouraged by the little profit they had gained. Rebellion was in their air. They clamored for Spain.

Turning back into storms, they were wrecked on the coast of Jamaica. Here two sailors—Mendez, a Castilian, and a Genoese named Fiesche—volunteered to make the journey to Española in a small-boat, to obtain supplies.

Meanwhile, the delay and the privation they suffered had its effect on the tempers of the troupe. Factions arose. Diego de Porras, notary to the King, who had come to supervise and evaluate the pearls, gold and other treasure they had expected to find, was a leader in the revolt. Aided by his brother Francisco, commander of one of the cara-

THE CONQUERORS AMONG THE NATIVES.

FROM A SIXTEENTH CENTURY WOOD-CUT.

"And the population was so large that there was
no need for consideration. . . . Men gambled at dice
with their slaves for the stake; ten women could be
had in exchange for one good cheese; a bottle of wine
was the price of one."

236

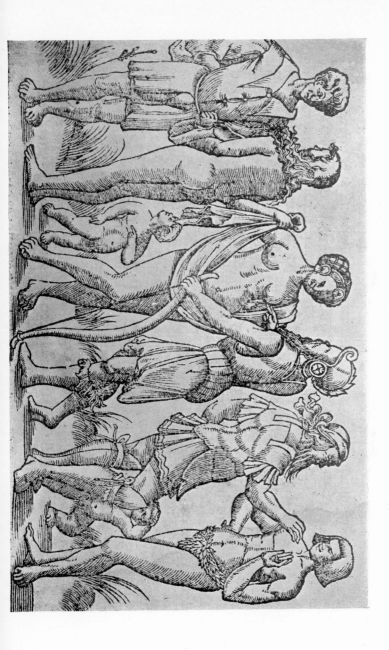

vels, and followed by a number of his friends from Seville, he took refuge on the island, making war both on the natives and on Columbus. In the end a pitched battle resulted between the two forces, in which Christopher had the advantage. The mutiny was quelled, and the deserters returned to their posts.

Eight months intervened, before word came from Española. At last a ship arrived, bringing a supply of provisions and a letter from Ovando, the Governor, expressing in the most courteous terms his regret that he must forbid the Admiral and Vice-Regent from setting foot in the colony.

As a matter of fact, conditions at Española were in far worse state now than those which had prompted Christopher's recall. Don Nicolas de Ovando had embarked on a veritable massacre of the natives. At the moment of writing to Columbus, eighty-four *caciques* had been burned or hung by his orders, and their chattels divided among the Spaniards, according to the system of *repartimiento*.

The *repartimiento* had been developed into the most utter and brutal system of slavery. The Queen, shocked by the report of Columbus' handling of her dark-skinned subjects, had issued the most precise and formal commands for the improvement of their condition. They were to be treated as freemen, and paid as such for their labors. They were to be instructed in the Christian religion, and to that end must be allowed rest from all work on Sundays. But the rapacity of the Governor and his associates had speedily found means to circumvent these provisions.

Actual slavery was replaced by more brusk and summary treatment. To the privileged, the Governor issued order-slips, signed by his hand—"I authorize you to enroll as many Indians as you may need to work, under the supervision of their *cacique* in your mine." The very vagueness of the wording gave the bearer of such a document unlimited authority.

Whole villages could be—and were—conscripted. Once set to work, death was the only release. The colonists, men used to the bitter life of the field or the prison camp, treated their slaves with the utmost savagery. The difference in language did not hinder them; a cord pickled in brine—called the "eel" in the prison slang of the day—served as a fluent interpreter. And the population was so large that there was no need for consideration; a man goaded to death could easily be replaced. Men gambled at dice with their slaves for the stake; ten women could be had in exchange for one good cheese; a bottle of wine was the price of one.

And to justify these cruelties, a whole system of false accusations were brought against the miserable people. They were charged with vices, ranging from sodomy to cannibalism—of both which they seem to have been equally

238

guiltless. These baseless accusations found their way into literature; engravings illustrating books which described the New World showed the Indians grouped around primitive altars, decorated with human heads and hands, or officiating at a ceremony by which captives were roasted alive on a grill.

The truth was quite opposite. The unnatural vice of sodomy develops always as the result of an unnatural repression of the normal sex instinct. In Spain, where the moral code was exceptionally severe, its practice was combated with the utmost rigor; as a crime, it was held to be worse than murder, and second only to heresy. Thus the charge, when brought against the natives, gave countenance to the penalties the colonists inflicted on them. As a matter of fact, they were ignorant of the vice.

With them, as with many primitive peoples, the custom of marriage had no strict definitions. Women were free to all members of the tribe. Virginity was considered almost a mark of shame, so that the tribesmen often refused to take a virgin for wife. Under such free conditions sodomy, of course, was unheard of.

As for the other charge, it seems abundantly established that the islanders, far from being cannibals, were in fact vegetarians. The sole exception to this régime was the dog, which, when roasted fat, and young, was the ceremonial feast of their banquets, a delight to the native gourmets.

However much the prospect of baked puppy-dog may revolt us, it certainly does not imply the barbarity of cannibalism, advanced against the natives by the colonists. Though this charge, like the others, was made chiefly as a salve to the conscience of the whites, it is possible that it may have had its beginning in misapprehension. Part of the religious practice of the natives grew out of their reverence for their ancestors. Like many other island tribes, they were accustomed to preserve the heads of their great men, dried and shrunk, in their council halls, and the horror of marauding white men, entering such a museum, may have led them to believe themselves among man-eaters.

Whether honestly or otherwise, these charges and many others were advanced, and expiated, more or less brutally, in slavery. Inadvertently, sometimes, the recital of native crime defeats itself and gives a pathetic picture of the actual condition. Thus we learn that, through an excess of deviltry, whole tribes, on learning that the Spaniards were approaching, would deliberately commit suicide by eating plants known to be poisonous. In other cases, captured Indians, stubborn before regeneration, would waste away and die by the mere will to live no longer, so great was their repugnance to the Christian rule.

Such instances as these, solemnly reported by the Spaniards themselves, give more clearly than any other, a picture of the despair that swallowed the natives, and the utter lack of understanding governing the whites.

In theory, of course, the Church was charged with the conversion and instruction of the Indians, and many of the priests were sincere in the effort to improve their condition, some even going so far as to refuse absolution to men known to have tortured their slaves. Their work, however, in the early greedy days, was of little avail.

Among these priests, the most important was Bartholomew de Las Casas—"The Father of the Indians." His father, a descendant of a family of Limoges, had sailed with Christopher on his first voyage. The son, upon the conclusion of his studies at the University of Seville, followed the Admiral on the third journey.

Entered in the Dominican Order, he spent the remainder of his life in the colonies, striving to alleviate the condition of the Indians, which he stated to be "the most bitter and horrible ever suffered either by man or beast." Of the early Spaniards he observed, "If the devil had a hoard of gold, the Spaniards would attack him to obtain it."

And it was he who, in 1542, appearing before the Council of Charles V, described the result of the long oppression in the most fearless condemnation:

"So now the Islands of Cuba and Jamaica are almost entirely barren and their population destroyed; likewise bereft of all living creature are the Lucayan Islands, which were so fertile and delightful that even the least one of them was more beautiful than the King's Gardens at Seville, and which numbered, at one time, more than fifty thousand inhabitants."

From the Council, hoping to save the land from ruin, he obtained permission to repopulate the Antilles with Negroes brought from Africa; later, in 1552, he published his "Short Relation of the destruction of the Indies," asserting that "a description of these atrocities would make a book to horrify the world."

His work was hopeless. By the very colonial system of Spain, which offered no pay to its emigrants, but forced them to exploit the natives, the slavery and brutality was made inevitable. So Cervantes described the Indies as "a refuge for those who had failed in Spain, an asylum for bankrupts, a safe harbor for murderers and tricksters and a haven for immoral women."

That such a population should have detested the Admiral is rather an honor to his name. There were, however, some few who remained faithful to him. One of these, Diego de Salcedo, formerly Christopher's equerry, had obtained in 1499 the concession to the sale of soap and perfumes in the Indies. Now, with a gratitude the more touching for the rapacity of the others, he loaded a caravel with provisions and set out to the rescue of his shipwrecked leader. Even then, it was a year before the stranded expedition could get under way again. Before undertaking the ocean crossing, they were forced to touch at Española.

So now, on the very spot where twelve years earlier he had first unfurled the flag of Spain, Christopher arrived, penniless, spent and weakened by age and hardship, and unwelcome. Don Nicolas de Ovando received him with the cold and exquisite courtesy of the grandee, but his enmity was apparent in his every attitude. Columbus had felt prison-chains once about his ankles. He made haste to get out on the open sea again.

The crossing, this time, was terrible, but the skies that lowered over them were no darker than Christopher's thoughts. Three times he had embarked, and three times returned, having sought and failed to find his *El Dorado*. And now again for the fourth time he confronted the archaic riddle of the west, and was returning to face a greater shame, a deeper ignominy, a sparser poverty than before.

The wind blew; foam piled over the forward decks; the wind whipped through the rigging, shattering their masts. "Never have I seen a storm of such duration as this one," he wrote.

Everything was slipping from his hands. Since Lisbon, there had been a gradual accumulation—the love of a noble lady, wealth, power, the increase of his knowledge and his ambition, his two sons born to him—all culminat-

243

ing with that first stubborn, relentless thrust westward that had borne him on to San Salvador and the discovery of the western lands. Since then, there had been a gradual dispersion of these benefits that had come to him. Four times he had thrust, stubborn still, to pierce the barrier of disillusion that lay across his path, abandoning all else to attain his one ambition. Of the two women who had given him his sons one was dead, the other he had put aside from his course. And for the rest: the rank and title, the glory of his name, the profits of his adventure? All had been swept away, as if by the winds of the ocean.

"Such is my fate," he wrote, "that the twenty years of service through which I passed, undergoing so much toil and danger, have gained me nothing, so that this very day I do not possess a roof in Spain which I can call my own; if I need to eat or sleep, there is nowhere to go but to the inns and taverns, and lack the money for the reckoning."

So broken by gout and years and suffering but still with almost insane persistence dreaming of fame and favor still to be won, Christopher's fourth attempt to reach the Indies ended in failure. On November 7, 1504, the weather-beaten caravel dropped anchor in the port of San Lucar, and its worn commander knelt at the altar of Our Lady of Charity, where the seventeen lamps still burned and the little silver ship still hung, votive offerings for his previous voyage.

XI. VALLADOLID

H E spent two weeks at Seville, recuperating, then prepared to visit the Court. It was winter, and freezingly cold for a man who had just come from the southern seas. To make the journey across Spain, the canons of the Seville Cathedral suggested that he go in a litter, carried by his servants, and offered to lend him the one in which the Cardinal Mendoza had been carried to his grave. Columbus agreed and gave a receipt for the richly-upholstered affair; as it turned out, however, he was not destined to recline on the cushions where the noble lover of Beatriz de Bobadilla had lain. In the midst of his preparations, terrible news came from the Court—news that struck both at his heart and his ambitions.

The Queen was dying. She was at Medina del Campo, with her household, in the great red brick castle which rises above the little town. She lay there, clad in the habit of the third order of Saint Francis, dying slowly of an intestinal tumor and refusing, from modesty, even to permit her doctors to diagnose the malady.

She had been some time ailing. Now, while the whole nation mourned, she was adding a codicil to her will, forbidding that her body be profaned by the hand of the embalmer, and when at last, during the administration of extreme unction, the bed-coverings were withdrawn to expose her feet, she instinctively pulled them back in place again, to conceal her nudity. And so, on November 26, 1504, she died.

"My hand," says Peter Martyr, "falls powerless by my side, for very sorrow." The whole nation shared his grief. No time was lost, as a consequence of her provision against embalming, in organizing the funeral cortege which was to transport the body to Granada. Hardly had it started, however, before terrific storms swept the country; bridges were washed away; roads were rutted and impassable. While the weary procession struggled on, the nation read all manner of portents in the tempest.

Her death was a more real omen to the Admiral, but even above his own interest in the matter he grieved sincerely for the Queen who had always trusted and believed in him. "It is our chief duty," he wrote to his son Diego, "to commend to God most affectionately and devotedly the soul of our dead lady, the Queen. Her life was ever Catholic and virtuous, and prompt to undertake all that could work in His service; wherefor we may believe she now rests in glory, far from all concern for this bitter and weary world."

Fernando had gone to join his elder brother, at the Court, Christopher remained, friendless and weak from gout, at Seville. "My dear son," he wrote in December to Diego, "I would that I might have letters from you every hour of the day; your judgment should tell you that now no other pleasure is given me."

Nevertheless, he hoped still to bring about a reconciliation with Fonseca. To this end, when he learned that the Indian Minister had been appointed Bishop of Valencia, he charged his son especially to offer his compliments to the dignitary. "If I come to the Court," he added, "I shall lodge at the home of His Grace, whether he be pleased or not, for thus I hope to renew our former friendship together."

At the moment, the Indian Ministry was in process of reorganization. Ovanda's administration, though cruel to the native, was profitable to Spain, and the Ministry was removed to larger quarters in the magnificent *Casa de Contratacion*—the Hall of Documents.

With the removal, Christopher's chance of winning back to favor grew less. The wry-headed Fonseca, cultured though he was and amateur in all the arts, had the pettiness of a slighted shop-girl in his treatment of those he hated.

CHRISTOPHER COLUMBUS AND HIS SONS DIEGO AND FERDINAND.

An engraving "from an ancient Spanish picture," the original of which is lost. It was painted perhaps in the period after his return from his last voyage, when he lay at Seville, recuperating, while he waited for a summons to the Court.

"All the privileges granted him were disregarded; the terms of the Capitulation which should have guaranteed him a magnificent income went completely unenforced."

He had not the breadth of nature to relent in animosity when a foe had fallen.

A greater enemy to Columbus' hopes than the spite of the newly-ordained Bishop, however, was the passage of time—the slow years that still moved faster than his caravels. Twelve years had passed since the discovery. A new generation had grown up, with new ideas and new intentions, and disdain for those of their elders. And never has a former hero been cast aside more suddenly and completely than the sea-weary veteran, Columbus.

He lay alone at Seville, and there was no one even to rail at him any more; he had simply been forgotten. Some years later, the painter Alejo Fernandez was commissioned to decorate the *Casa de Contratacion*; he painted an altarpiece, which remains now in the Alcazar, the painting called popularly *La Virgen de los Conquistadores*—The Virgin of the Conquerors.

The painting shows a tranquil harbor, where rides a fleet of caravels and galleons, great ships and small, of all the kinds which were used by the discoverers of the western world. And these, Cortez, Balboa, Pizarro and the rest, are portrayed kneeling in devotion while above them the Virgin floats smiling in the sky.

But among them all, the close observer will note that one face is missing—that of Columbus, the man who led the way in which all the others followed. Christopher had simply been forgotten.

And now the confidence of the Court and the glory of renown had been usurped by the younger men. Amerigo Vespucci, Vicente-Iañez Pinzon—brother of Columbus' first associate—Hojeda and Juan de la Cosa—his former aids and lieutenants—these were the men who now commanded the colonial fleets. In that same year, young Cortez emigrated to Española, the first step along the way that was to lead him into the palace of Montezuma. Nine years later, Vasco Nuñez de Balboa would ride his horse down the beach into the waters of the Pacific, waving his flag in token of possession, and by his discovery reversing ideas of the world's form that had obtained since the time of Ptolemy. Such men as these had taken Christopher's place in the glory of the day. One—Amerigo Vespucci—was to usurp a share of his glory in history.

Vespucci was the son of a notary in Florence. He made his beginnings in the counting rooms of the Medicis, was soon transferred to their Spanish branch, and became eventually a partner in the firm of Juanoto Berardi, shipbuilders and traders. If the impulse that made Columbus an explorer was ambition, that of Vespucci was more simply greed.

It is possible that the two had met before during Hojeda's visit to Española. At any rate, when the Florentine returned from a later voyage to the islands and discovered that Columbus lay at Seville, he made haste to approach him and seek his friendship. The welcome he received from the deserted Admiral may easily be imagined.

Soon after, when Vespucci left for Segovia, he carried with him a letter of introduction to Diego, committing him to the full confidence of the son. "He showed ever the desire to make himself agreeable to me," Christopher wrote. "He is an extremely accomplished man, though his fate has so far thwarted him as it has so many others; so far his success has not been what his merits deserve. He leaves me, full of good friendship for me." And the last letter which remains today, written by the Admiral, ends with the sentence: "I have sent word to you by Amerigo Vespucci." It was the irony of fate that this friend and compatriot was involuntarily to rob Columbus of great measure of his glory. The event was the purest accident.

Vespucci had a fondness for the pen; he drew up a recital of each of his voyages in the form of a letter addressed to one or another of the great personages of the day. One such letter, describing the western continent, was sent to René, Duke of Lorraine. He gave it to his secretary, Gautier Lud.

Lud was a member of a learned society called the Lyceum of the Vosges; he read the letter to his colleagues. It so interested them that in 1507 they published it, together with an "Introduction to Cosmography" written by a member of the society, Martin Waltzenmuller of Saint-Dié, nicknamed Hylacomylus.

Until this event, the regions discovered by Columbus had been designated as *Terra Sancte Crucis sive Mondus Novus* —"The Land Of The Sainted Cross, otherwise The New World." It was by this title that it is called in the epitaph of the Genoese, Pope Innocent VIII.

Waltzenmuller, however, flattered to be published in collaboration with the distinguished explorer, repaid the debt by christening the continent after him. In his "Introduction" he remarked: *"Quarta orbis pars quam quia Americus invenit, Amerigen quasi Americi terram sine Americam nun cupare licet"*—In extent one-fourth of the globe (which, since Americus discovered it, might permissibly be called Amerigen, as to say Land of Americus, or American Land). The name he proposed was simpler, and took the public fancy. And the studious burgher of Saint-Dié became god-father to a continent to which Columbus' name might more rightfully have been given. It is so given now only on the rare occasions when, not very logically, we sing of it as the "gem of the ocean."

Meanwhile, Columbus felt only the sincerest gratitude to Vespucci, for his kindness to him, in his loneliness. His finances, as well as his friends, had been cut away from him. All the privileges granted him were disregarded; the terms of the Capitulation which should have guaranteed him a magnificent income went completely unenforced. Even the pensions and other payments accorded him came late and lapsed often, and all his complaints to the King met with no response. At last, in 1505, he decided to go in person to the Court, then lying at Segovia.

And here another difficulty presented itself. The hard winter had sapped his strength; he found himself no longer able to control the gait of a horse. But for some time, the King had been concerned at a tendency among his nobles to abandon the breeding of horses in preference for the less costly and more enduring mule. If this continued, a war might find him without a cavalry. According, a decree had been issued, limiting the use of the mule to church-men and women. All others must travel horseback.

So Christopher was again delayed, while a dispensation was sought for him from the King, permitting him to make the journey by mule. The spring of the year was well ad-vanced before, at last, he presented himself before the Court, at Segovia.

Ferdinand received him with the greatest courtesy, pro-testing his affection for his servant, even deigning to offer the royal solicitude and sympathy on the subject of the Admiral's gout. His words, however, were not seconded by actions. Each time Christopher presented himself at the palace, he was met with the same consideration—and was sent away with the same empty pockets.

The King assured him, as Herrera reports "that he fully estimated his important services and, far from stinting his recompense to the precise terms of the Capitulation, intended to confer more ample favors on him in Castille." But the rewards and favors remained unpaid. In the meantime, the grateful monarch ordered the sale of Christopher's effects left at Española, and the sequestration of his share of the revenue from the colonies—the whole to be paid into the royal treasury, in order to meet the debts which the Admiral had contracted.

To Ferdinand, astute as he was in the art of intrigue, such dealings would appear only in the light of prudence and balance in the administration of the kingdom. When Columbus had first appeared in Spain, he had seemed but a ragged visionary, offering, for the mere scratch of a pen, to risk his life in the search of an imaginary treasure-land. Under such conditions, Ferdinand seemed to have nothing to lose by acceding to the man's demands; it had been much as if Columbus had said, "Will you give me one-tenth of the moon, if I bring it back to you?"

But the lands distant as the moon had been shown to be attainable. And now, as the gold from the mines Ovando so cruelly exploited came in greater and greater quantity; as each succeeding voyage showed the land of Christopher's vice-regency to be broader and broader in extent, the full magnitude of the concessions he had guaranteed to their discovery was borne in on the mind of the King. He saw that, once the conditions of the Capitulation were observed, Columbus would become at one bound the wealthiest and most powerful nobleman in the land.

To a man of Ferdinand's temperament, there could be only one result possible in such a situation. Crafty, grasping and overweening himself, he read Christopher's ambition as greed, his protestations of loyalty as dissimulation, and his daring as a longing for power. Give the Admiral the wealth and control in the colonies which the contract called for, and he would surely want more. The King was fond of proverbs, and probably his favorite was whatever might have been the Spanish equivalent of: "Give him an inch and he'll take an ell." He had no intention of permitting Christopher to take even the introductory inch.

Columbus, involved in his mysticism but blunt and sincere to a fault in dealing with men, could have no comprehension of so intricate a process of mind. At last, in bitterness, he came to know what treatment he could expect at the King's hands, but he went to his death without understanding why.

For the time, his hopes remained strong. Failing at Segovia, he followed on his mule when the Court removed to Salamanca. Snatching at straws, and imagining thus to disarm the strange suspicion with which he knew himself to be regarded, he proposed to renounce all advantage and privilege in the Indies—vice-regency, profit, admiralty, everything, investing all in the name of his son Diego—if only his projects might be realized. He could not understand that the King's attitude toward him had nothing of personal malevolence in its character. He could not conceive that the King's eye watched him, weighed his actions, probed his purpose with the same cold, impassive unfeeling as that with which he scrutinized the politics of Italy and Flanders, or studied the movement of intrigue among his own nobles.

The Court moved on, to Valladolid. Christopher followed.

Valladolid lies in a cleft among barren, treeless mountains; a silent city, a city of convents, and drowsy streets, and dusty buildings ornamented with the lions of Castille, where the court chancellories sleep at their functions. Columbus dropped from his weary mule in the inn-yard of the town and consigned the animal to the stables which occupied the ground floor. At the side, a narrow door, similar (and perhaps the thought crossed his mind) to that inn-door on the *via del Mulcento*, gave access to the rooms reserved for travellers. The façade, however, was typical of the Spanish tavern: large windows, each opening on a balcony, with dormer windows cutting the overhanging roof. He took quarters on the second floor.

His room was poor, ill-furnished; it was all he could afford. He hung on the wall the chains which he carried with him as a reminder of man's ingratitude ever since they had been struck from his limbs. He cut a hole in the planking of the floor, through which he could look down into the stable below, and watch his mule. And here, with his gout, his bitterness, and the faded remembrance of his glory, lived Christopher Columbus, by grant of their Most Catholic Majesties Ferdinand and Isabella the "Lord Admiral of the Ocean Sea, Vice-Regent and Governor over all islands and continents there discovered and acquired, and beneficiary to the tenth part of such profit as the commerce and traffic with these islands and continents may return; by right entitled to preëminences and privileges equal to those enjoyed by the Grand Admiral of Castille" . . .

If sometimes such snatches of the document his Sovereigns had signed in their camp at Santa Fé before Granada came back to him, there were other memories as well. Now the very silence of Valladolid made more real the sounds and scenes through which his destiny had driven him.

He remembered Genoa, the twisting tumult of its upper streets, and the sea's sounds and the creak of ships' stays, in the harbor. He remembered Lisbon: heard again the choir in the convent chapel of Santos where he had prayed, heard the marriage rite performed and smelled the myrtle wreath his young wife Felipa had worn. He heard the cry of Beatriz, in love's desperation. He remembered the light that winked in the darkness, and the emerald vision at dawn, and heard the cannon speak and the men cry all together, announcing land.

He heard the beat of native drums and the strange call of tropical birds; and that rose into the blare of trumpets ushering him through Spain and into Barcelona, the whole city delirious with joy; he saw the Kings again, smiling at him, in his triumph . . . and he was alone again, in the silence at Valladolid.

Night falls; the city goes from its day's siesta to its night of sleep. Windows are shuttered. The river runs softlier beneath the bridges. Murderers seek forgiveness in the little chained space where they are granted asylum by the Dominicans in the Church of San Pablo. Wayfarers vanish from the streets.

Christopher kneels to the planking to peer down at his mule, chewing his oats in the stable below. The silence hums in his ears, the silence of Valladolid, like that of eternity. And the bed is made, and he sleeps.

But Ferdinand had not forgotten him; the King had been watching. He watched his landless Governor, his impoverished Grand Admiral sink deeper into penury, and waited for the auspicious moment. At last, when he felt that poverty had bitten deep enough into the man's ambition, he acted. Word came to Christopher that, if he agreed to relinquish all claim to the privileges guaranteed him by the Capitulation, the King would grant him in return a comfortable estate situated in the Province of Leon, the domain of Carrion de los Condes. "Half a loaf is better than no bread," was perhaps another of the King's aphorisms.

But Christopher was of the sort who will abate not one crumb of their rights. He refused. And once more he was left alone again, with his chains, his mule, his maps and his mystic books.

Once, in another day, he had told Doña Juana de Torre of his plan to sail to the northern pole; he was convinced that the inhabitants of that region were endowed with a strange endurance. They died, he thought, only by their own desire, when they had had enough of living. Now, it seemed, he himself had almost had enough of life. He grew weaker.

On May 19, 1506 he called for a notary, Pedro de Hinojedo. To him, and in the presence of his confessor Gaspar de la Misericorda, he confirmed the conditions of the will drawn by his hand a year earlier, together with the conditions of the *mayorazgo* he had instituted in 1502, copy of which had been deposited at the Chartreuse monastery of Las Cuevas. The testament was witnessed by the Captain

259

Bartolomeo Fiesche, Andrea de Mirueña, a student, and six servants of the household.

At the same time, he added a codicil addresed to Diego:

"I do request and command of my son Diego that he have in his care Beatriz Enriquez, mother of my son Don Fernando, and I desire that he shall provide for her in such manner that she may live honorably, as one to whom I owe much. May this be done for the easement of my conscience, because my soul is burdened with a great weight. It would not be seemly for me to give here the reason."

He included a series of small legacies—"to be distributed in such way that the beneficiaries may not know from whom they come"—apparently either in restitution or in gratitude. Among the persons named are the heirs of Girolamo del Porto, the creditor in bankruptcy of his father; Antonio Bazo, a Genoese trader of Jewish birth, who had lived near the ghetto gates in Lisbon; the descendants of his early employers: Luigi Centurione Scoto, Paolo di Negri, and the son-in-law of Centurione, Battista Espinola, who had lived at Lisbon in 1482.

Though he made ready for death, he did not expect it to come so soon. A new hope had arisen to excite him. The heirs of Isabella, Philip the Good and his consort Joana, were on their way to take the throne of Castille. Columbus hoped they might inherit, too, the Queen's favorable opinion of him; he wrote at once for aid and a chance to prove his service, and sent his brother Bartholomew to offer them his compliments. The princely pair arrived, in a dazzle of brilliance the more striking for the tragedy that was to follow on their folly. They had no time for Columbus' plea. The clamor of their welcome drowned out the little cry that came from the inn at Valladolid.

Christopher died on May 20, 1506, still reaching for the attainment of his dream.

Like his Queen, he died wearing the habit of the third order of Saint Francis; a few friends, and several fathers of the Franciscan Order watched his end. He was buried in their monastery at Valladolid, and his chains were buried with him, according to his desire. The Court Historians, in the past, had had much to say of his discoveries and his triumphs. Now three lines served as his obituary in the record of Peter Martyr d'Anghera.

Several years later, his body was removed from Valladolid to Seville, and interred in the Chartreuse Chapel of Santa Maria de la Cuevas. This time there was pomp and ceremonial. While his remains were laid away beneath the cypress trees along the Guadalquivir, the King himself was present at the Cathedral, in solemn service. The dignitaries of the *Casa de Contratacion* knelt with their sovereign, while the burial rite was performed. If the marble was cold and hard to their knees, it was not as cold, nor as hard, as the irons they had rivetted on him whom now they mourned.

While Christopher lay in the Chapel of Cuevas, his ancient enemy, Don Juan de Fonseca was buried beneath the nave of the Church of Santa Maria, at Coca. A magnificent sarcophagus covered, and still covers, his tomb. His effigy is there, carved by the sculptor Bartolome Ordoñez; one may see the narrow forehead, haughty nose, the determined chin and thick-tufted brows perpetuated in the marble.

The face is hard and unbeautiful; the expression is bitter, even in death. And bitterness had come to him. The man who blocked Columbus and hindered Magelhaes met his master at last in Cortez. The conqueror of Mexico was a hard-bitten soldier, warier than Christopher; he possessed, in addition, an unfailing talisman to the favor of the Crown—the treasures of Montezuma that Christopher himself had failed by so little of discovering. When Fonseca sought to impose his will on Cortez, and the two men clashed, and the decision came to the Emperor, he pronounced unhesitatingly against his Minister. Don Juan retired, to die in disgrace and humiliation.

The cemetery at Cuevas was not destined to be the final resting-place of the great traveller. In the first half of the sixteenth century, Doña Maria de Toledo, his posthumous daughter-in-law, exhumed his body and carried it to Santo-Domingo, where it was buried in the choir of the Cathedral.

Later, in 1795, when Haiti was lost to the Spanish rule, the Governor could not bear to leave to the newcomers the body of the man whom, while alive, the whole nation had abandoned. The body was again exhumed, and transported to Havana, and again buried.

Here, in the passage of time and by the effect of earthquake and neglect, the casket was so shattered that, when at last the grave was opened, the bones of the great Admiral and those of the unillustrious others buried in the same cavern were found to be mingled and confused.

Time had passed and changes worked in the colonies as well. Whips swung between-decks in the galleons, and the heavy-laden ships moved past the coral reefs and down out of the harbors as the native rowers bent to the oars. Whips swung in the mine-workings, and the natives labored with pick and shovel, following the glint of gold. Whips swung in the plantation fields, and the natives sowed and hoed and garnered, and the crops of cane, cotton and tobacco were harvested.

But time passed, piling up the centuries, and out of that strange and bloody mixture of courage and adventure, suffering, self-sacrifice, brutality, idealism, blindness and clear vision, the nations of two continents rose to wealth and grandeur.

EPILOGUE
THE CASA SOLAR

Don Fernando wept for his father, in the manner befitting to a dutiful and affectionate son. The former page in the Queen's household was above all things a student of the proprieties. At the time, too, a taste for things literary was held to be not unbecoming in a younger son. In this respect, his own leanings agreed with the fashion: Don Fernando paid his court to the realm of letters.

Duty to the King was not neglected, and the King, in return, so far honored him as to employ him on several important missions. On one of these, he was sent to oversee the foundation of several churches and monasteries in the Antilles. Don Fernando marked out on a fair clean chart the sites he had chosen for the construction of the religious buildings, and sent it back to the King. What reward he had in Heaven for these labors we know not; his immediate recompense from his Sovereign was the gift of four hundred native slaves, and the fruit of their toiling was welcome, for it gave him leisure to pursue his studies.

And in truth, this dabbling in things literary which he had begun as the purest dilettante ended as almost his ruling passion. Books he collected lovingly. On the fly-leaf of each volume he wrote his name, and the date, place and price of the purchase. So great a reader could not but write, as well. Don Fernando was the author of many subtle Latin verses; nor did he disdain the more vulgar tongues, as proved by the villanelles he dashed off in the castilian.

His chosen study remained, however, that of history—which has been called the vindication of kings—and after history, genealogy—the study by which one strives to provide as many illustrious ancestors as possible for the important people of the day.

Among the names whose genealogies he studied, Don Fernando found the greatest difficulty with his own. Innumerable, he discovered, were the Colons, Coulons, Colombs, Colombis, Collomps whose armorial bearings were listed with the heralds. But none had furnished the name, however spelled, with a glory of achievement at all comparable to that of the Vice-Regent of the Indies. And it was, manifestly, impossible that so great a hero could have been of other than the highest birth.

Don Fernando plunged deeper, losing himself in a kind

of labyrinthine pigeon-coop of blazonry, wandering among doves, pigeons and martlets, in various number and variously disposed on the field: among birds in all attitudes, close, rising, volant; among coats original, coats dimidiated, differenced and impaled. And of all those bearing the dove for charge, the oldest and most honorable seemed to be that of the Counts of Cuccaro, in Montferrat: azure, and three doves argent.

In their case, the name of Colombo could be traced back to the tenth century and the reign of the Emperor Othon II, and back even further still, until it vanished in the mists of antiquity. Don Fernando inclined to believe that his father derived from their branch of the name. But first he must make sure. The then chieftains of the family, though over ninety years of age, had the greatest reputation for sagacity. Their proposed relative decided to visit and consult with them on the matter.

The journey was made, of course, in the manner befitting a grandee of Spain, master of four hundred slaves. Don Fernando travelled in search of an ancestry with torchmen, footmen and lackeys; he rode in a luxurious coach, drawn by four mules.

The *casa solar* he sought—the ancestral mansion of the Counts of Cuccaro—turned out to be a square-built castle constructed in the style affected by Bramante, the great Italian architect of the previous century. A line of carven

266

columns, forming an arcade, alone relieved its simple severity. Above the portal, three doves, in weather-stained marble, intertwined their beaks.

As he approached, a crowd of villagers swarmed about his coach and ran on before to the castle, to announce his coming, and the aged Counts themselves, wrinkled and stooped, came first to their window and then to the castle-gate, to greet him.

Old as they were, these Colombos had something of the impenetrable smooth polish of the Italian in their manner. Don Fernando was received with all the courtesy due his rank, yet their deference was tinged with irony and defiance for his Spanish birth.

His good breeding, however, soon set them at their ease. After the fashion of travellers, he furnished them first with all the news he had heard along the way. Then, delicately, he touched upon the subject of his search. Was he, by chance, a relative of theirs?

Age, in respect to their family at least, had in no wise dulled the edge of memory in the two Counts of Cuccaro. To be sure, piled high in the *soffita*—the garret of the castle —were reams on reams of documents, establishing their family tree. They were left there, undisturbed, to the dust and the rats. The Colombos of Montferrat knew well that this Spanish pretender had no place in their lineage. With gentle irony, they excused themselves on the ground of age, which had led them so utterly to forget their connection with the distinguished Spanish visitor. Don Fernando, dissatisfied, departed.

Neither he nor they could have imagined that in a later day a grand-son of the proud Counts was to come, in his turn, pleading alliance with this Spaniard they despised. Yet such was the outcome of this strange comedy. When the last male descendent of the Admiral, Don Cristobal de Colon, died in 1583 without issue, the first to appear before the Indian Ministry was Baldassare Colombo, Count of Cuccaro, claiming the inheritance of the estate.

The justification this gentleman had constructed was even more fantastic than those of Don Fernando's imagining. According to his tale, Christopher and Bartholomew, as children, had strayed from the castle of Cuccaro. Wandering to Genoa, they were adopted by the others there, and had grown up unknowing of their heritage, until the visit of Don Fernando had revived a memory of the matter. His story made the Admiral a kind of male Cinderella, or a sea-going Tom Thumb, but the many discrepancies did not appear in so clear a light as now. It was only by the narrowest of margins that the Count of Cuccaro, descendant of the Crusaders, did not win the honor of relationship with the weaver's son of Genoa!

Don Fernando, failing at Cuccaro, set forth for Genoa, and arrived there the following evening.

The ancient city had not changed since his father's departure. It lay still secure in its circle of hills and its ring of fortifications, with its masts and towers rising above the walls. If change there had been, it was only that the watchtowers had grown older, and the gold in the coffers of the Banca di San Giorgio more deeply piled. Don Fernando entered by the Gate of San Andrea, and proceeded down the *via del Mulcento*, with his torchmen lighting the path which his lackeys, shouting in the name of the Emperor, cleared before him.

In a small house by the roadside, where Bianchinetta Colombo and her husband Bavarello had sliced and sold their cheeses, the son Pantalino sat drinking and talking with his cronies of the neighborhood. The bottle passed, and for the hundredth time the host recounted the tale of his marvellous uncle, who had discovered the islands of the Indies, and had been made an Admiral by the King of Spain. For the hundredth time, his story was greeted with shouts of laughter.

"Why doesn't he come to see you, Pantalino?" they cried. "Where is this magical Admiral of yours? Let us see him, for once!"

As they spoke, they heard shouts and unaccustomed noises in the street—the rattle of hoofs, the clink of chains and the cries of torch-bearers. Still laughing, they crowded to the door.

Lit by the light of his torches, swept on by the rush of his coachmen, they saw a laced and brocaded nobleman, lying back among the cushions of his carriage, proudly unaware of the clamoring crowd. A moment, and he had passed, the lights and tumult dying toward the town. Pantalino went back to his cheeses. Don Fernando rode on, quite unaware that he had passed the very threshold of his *casa solar*.

Next day, however, he did not fail to pay his respects to the gentlemen of the *Signoria*, and the Directors of the Banca di San Giorgia. He was received with the utmost courtesy, and the consideration due a man of influence with the Emperor, who might use that influence in favor of the city. But though more willing, these gentlemen were able to do no more to aid Don Fernando's search than had the Counts of Cuccaro.

If they mentioned the subject of the Admiral's bequest, concerning the reduction of the tax on wine and wheat, it was but glancingly. Genoa had been made aware of the parsimony of Don Diego, Don Fernando's elder brother. And the Republic was rich enough to disdain insistence. It may not, perhaps, have been so well with the objects of that other condition of the *mayorazgo*, by which the Admiral ordained a comfortable pension to be paid in support of a member of the family, settled at Genoa. If paid at all, we can be sure it was made out, not to the humble Pantalino, but to one more presentable, perhaps the Capitano Giovanni Antionio, or some one of his brothers.

So Don Fernando returned to Spain, a little cooled, perhaps, in his ardor for genealogical research. But if patents of nobility were lacking to his collection, there was no lack of books. His coach was heavy-laden with gems from the Italian book-shops, on the return.

But the journey had bred in him a love for travel, though his trips were made usually without the discomforts that had marked those of his father. In 1515, he returned again to Genoa. It is possible that this time his humble cousin Pantalino made effort to approach him. It is more likely, however, that the poor cheesemonger would regard his arrival with much the same awe and divine superstition in which the natives held the Admiral, landing at San Salvador. Certainly, Don Fernando was left undisturbed with the castles in Spain and out of it his imagination was building.

Meantime, his rise in the favor of the Emperor Charles V had been constant. The Emperor took him as companion to Aix-la-Chapelle. Here, certainly, at the brilliant coronation, Don Fernando could enjoy to surfeiting his taste for the society of the high-born. Following this, he was appointed Court Cosmographer; he received several richly-paid pensions. Don Diego, his elder brother, was married to the Doña Maria de Toledo, whose blood held a strain of the blood of the Emperor.

Don Diego, unlike his brother, led a dull and uneventful life. To a man of his parsimonious temperament, the greatest adventure of his career was a loan of ten thousand ducats made to the Emperor, on the eve of his coronation. Diego died in 1526.

His death revealed that he had at least one quality in common with his father and his grandfather. He was slow in paying his debts. Don Diego could lend a fortune to his Emperor, but his will passed on to his heirs settlement of the same anonymous legacies which, seventeen years earlier, his father has passed on to him.

At the death of Don Diego, Fernando made every effort to protect the inheritance of Don Luiz, Diego's son. But the chief occupation of the Court Cosmographer was the supervision of the mansion which he was building, near the Gate of Hercules, at Seville. He spared no effort to make it beautiful.

Sculptors from Genoa were imported to carve the detail of its façade. The garden, sloping down to the banks of the Guadalquivir, was planted with exotic trees and flowers, brought from the western isles. Their perfume, when the wind was right, carried across the river, to the chapel of Cuevas, where lay the body of the Admiral.

Here, among his tropic foliage, Don Fernando grew

older, following the pleasant musing way of the book-lover. He read and reread, arranged, catalogued and re-catalogued his library. In his calm, he had but one troubling thought: no Life of the Admiral had appeared, and was it not his duty to compile it? He had written verse and panegyric to celebrate his sovereigns; should he not devote some attention to his father?

An event occurred which strengthened his resolve. It was just at this time that the Dominican Agostino Giustiniani was publishing at Genoa the "Polyglot Psalter" to which we have some time ago referred. The qualification given to the Admiral—"ortus vilibus parentibus"—sprang from the page at Don Fernando's eyes. "Born of humble parents!" His father! His wrath set the spark to his enterprise.

Don Fernando set to work, turning over the papers of his father, his letters, the official documents he had treasured. He sought out the functionaries, the courtiers who had had to do with the Admiral. Fernando himself had accompanied Christopher on the last voyage, and he searched now in his mind for what hints his father might have dropped, in their conversations concerning his past. But Columbus himself, we know, had been quite willing to let the glory he arrived at eclipse his poor beginnings. He had revealed little to his son, the page in the Royal House.

There were those still living, however, who might have

told. There were the monks at Our Lady of La Rabida; there were those who remembered, among the townspeople of Palos. And he might certainly have found some hint of the truth at Lisbon, in the Genoese quarter, or among the mariners who had sailed with the Centurione.

There were all these, and there was another, whose love had refreshed the ragged and poverty-stricken dreamer, when first he came to the Court of Spain. But the Court Cosmographer, in those days, saw little of the mother from whose house he had gone to the Queen's. Beatriz Enriquez, as if her one year of love had marked the fulfilment of her destiny on earth, remained thereafter in the background, watching uncomplaining the rise, first of her lover, and later, of her son. She died, unknown, at an advanced age.

So it was natural that Don Fernando should see his father only as lighted by the brilliance of his discovery and the glitter of his titles. This light he reflected backward along the preceding years. Life at the Court, as well, had taught him that princes, like little children, can often embroider fact with imagination. In the end, he did the same. His great work, the famous *Historie del Almirante*— its full title, "The History of the Life and of the Discoveries of the Admiral Christopher Columbus"—emerges now as a sort of tapestry of glory, like those on which court-ladies weave the adventures, real or imaginary, of their monarch.

In it, the question of genealogy was the first he undertook to answer. The opening chapter considers all the ramifications of the matter. With generous forbearance, he refuses to accept as other than hearsay, the tradition that the family derived from the conqueror of Mithridates, the Consul Columbus, of Rome. On the other hand, he is scathing in condemnation of the "tissue of errors and misrepresentation" fabricated by Giustiniani. In the end, he relates his father to the Colombos of Piacenza, a family which, though poor, had given many great captains and two admirals to the Genoese Navy. In support of this contention, he quotes a rather negative assertion made by Christopher himself, in a letter to Doña Juana de Torre:

"I am not the first admiral of my name; let them call me by what title pleases them; David himself was a shepherd before he became King. I am the humble servant of the same God who watched over the destiny of David. . . ."

While Fernando worked on the *Historie,* the graceless monk Giustiniani burst into print again with his "Annals of the Republic of Genoa," in which he once more referred to the poor beginnings of the Admiral. With wrath increased, Don Fernando began the composition of a still sharper reply, to be included in the "Life." He was not, however, fated to complete it. In 1539, after a short illness, death called him from his desk. He was buried in the Cathedral of Seville.

The original manuscript, by the chance of time, has been lost. The earliest known text is the Italian translation, published at Venice in 1571, under the title: *Historie et vera relatione della vita e de' fatti del Ammiraglio D. Christoforo Colombo.*

His pretensions aside, Fernando seems to have been a pleasant and quite capable personage, and one of considerable attainment as a bibliophile. His library, at his death, numbered 15,370 volumes, perhaps the greatest collection of his day. And so Don Fernando de Colon, born in despair, died a trusted official at the Court of the Emperor, at the age of fifty-two years.

His nephew and heir, Don Luiz, son of Don Diego, received the title Duke of Veragua, on relinquishing, as Christopher had refused to do, all claim to the Vice-Regency of the Indies. He, too, was an ardent collector— more ardent even than Fernando for, instead of books, he collected wives, at one time marrying a third lady while two others remained to him. For this, it would seem a trifle tardily, he was thrown into prison. The story of his release and his captivity might have made matter for the opera bouffe.

Bribes freely given afforded him the freedom of the prison gates after dark. On one such sortie, a quarrel gained him a sword-wound that might have finished him. On another, though already burdened with three wives, the fancy took him to add another to his list. He married his mistress, Luisa de Carvajal. Some months later, freed from the prison, but exiled from the kingdom, he sailed to Oran, and died seven years later. In his will he designated as his heir the son born to him by the fourth wife, but the succession was contested. Sisters, step-sister, cousins and outsiders entered the lists, among others Baldassare Count of Cuccaro. In the end, the one already most powerful won the case, Nuño de Portugal, Count of Gelves. Four hundred thousand ducats were distributed among the others; two thousand ducats went to Baldassare,—a kind of royal reward for the vinegary greeting his grandfathers had given Don Fernando, almost a century before.

In 1711, the line of Nuño de Portugal ended; the dukedom of Veragua passed to his daughter's husband, James Francis Fitz-James Stuart, son of the Marshal of Berwick. Eventually, the duchy to which Christopher's Vice-Regency had shrunk was included in the appanages of the Duke of Alba, and so ended, as a separate title.

Thus Christopher, himself seeking a *casa solar*, was himself the founder of a family to which those he envied were proud to claim allegiance. So too, thinking to trace the way to the Indies, he endowed the world with two continents, a domain far richer than any treasure he had dreamed of finding.

He was a man of pertinacity, vision and endurance; a man stubborn in his ideals and mystic in his principles. The love of women and the motives of men seem alike to have been beyond his comprehension; he was at home only with the elements, and he returned from them to die, broken, ashore. In his cosmography, he judged rightly but guessed wrong, and the guess once made he wrecked his ships, his credit, his men, his health, his wealth, and finally his own life, in futile and persistent effort to prove it true.

While he lived, he had glory, honor and position within his grasp, and before he died, saw all fade and disappear. But after death, greater glory, greater honor and respect came to his name than ever he, living, could have hoped for.

APPENDIX

PORTRAITS OF COLUMBUS

"If his discovery of the New World," wrote Hererra, "had been made in the times of the Ancients, they would not only have built temples and statues in his honor; they would have named stars and constellations after him, as they did for Hercules and Bacchus."

Living when he did, it is doubtful if any authentic portrait of the Admiral remains.

Genoa, his place of birth, was not properly speaking a city peculiarly artistic. Had Christopher been born in Florence, for example, where the artists grew toward the people and the people toward art, and any poor man's child was fit subject for a masterpiece, his portrait while young might still have been drawn. But in the Republic—as so often happens with republics —art was reserved for the Church and the patrician. It is improbable that so humble a youth could have trespassed on so high a domain.

After his accession to the ranks of the mighty, much doubt still remains. On the return from the first voyage, he was a guest for some time at the royal palace, in Barcelona. Now, Isabella had a pronounced leaning for the arts. Numerous painters were constantly in her entourage: Francisco Chacon of Toledo, the Court Painter, as well as Antonio del Rincon and many foreign artists, such as Melchior Aleman, Miguel Flamenco, or Zittoz, who painted her portrait in 1481, and Juan de Flandes, who received in 1498 a grant of 30,000 maravedis from her hand. At her death, an inventory listed 460 paintings in her possession, of which a great part were immediately sold, chiefly to finance the construction of the royal chapel at Granada.

It is practically certain that, at the height of Christopher's fame, some one of the Court painters must have asked him to sit for a portrait. When the collection was sold, however, Columbus was in low repute and the work may very well have been painted over with another scene. It is an interesting and quite possible supposition that under the draperies and foliage of some fifteenth century canvas may be hidden the only authentic portrait of the Admiral.

It is odd too, that Don Fernando, ardently seeking all that pertained to his father, should not have uncovered a portrait if one existed. But the Queen's gallery was speedily dispersed. Many of the canvasses went immediately to Italy, where there was a vogue for the likenesses of famous personages. The galleries of the Bishop of Nocera had set the example, and the gentlemen of fashion followed it, until the hall of every pallazzo in Italy contained its row of portraits, ranging from Attila to the dukes and princes of the day.

Such a condition led inevitably to many artistic forgeries. Few of the portraits were authentic and many were copies. Thus a shadow is cast over the origins of that portrait of Columbus in the Nocera collection, which was copied in 1552 by Altissimo for the Duke Cosimo de Medicis. It bore the inscription: *Columbus Lygur. Novi Orbis. Reptor.*

The same portrait was again copied by Tobias Stimmer, and

an engraving published in the edition of the *Elogia virorum bellica virtute illustrium*, published by Perna in 1557 at Basle.

The authenticity of the portrait, at this date, can only be estimated by comparing the lineaments of the figure depicted with the descriptions given of the Admiral by his contemporaries. The Venetian, Angelo Trevisan, who saw Christopher in 1501, at Granada, describes him as "a man of tall and powerful stature, ruddy, spirited, and long-visaged."

"The Admiral came to Castille," wrote Barnaldez, Historian to the Kings, "in the month of June in the year 1496, clad in a cloak of the same color as worn by the Franciscan Brotherhood of the Observance, and wearing as a mark of devotion the rope girdle of Saint Francis."

He was described by his son Fernando as follows: "The Admiral was of more than the middle height, and of good proportion; his face was long, neither round nor lean, and the cheek-bones high. His nose was aquiline, the eyes clear and light-colored; his complexion was light, but grew sanguine easily in excitement. In youth, his hair was yellow, but whitened at the age of thirty."

It seems certain that, if a portrait of the Admiral were known to exist, Fernando would have mentioned it, to complete the description. And certainly the portrait of Nocera (now owned by one of his descendants, the Marchese Orchi of Rome) as well as the copy at Florence and the canvas attributed to Ridolfo Ghirlandaio now in the Civic Museum at Genoa are alike in that they give the impression of having been drawn from description, rather than at first hand. All reveal the same characteristics: a face of ordinary aspect, gray hair drawn back from the forehead, dark clothing—in short no trace of personal particularization.

The Duke of Parma, and after him the Cavaliere Rossi, owned

a painting, said to be a portrait of Columbus, by the hand of Lorenzo Lotti. This canvas later entered the collection of James W. Ellsworth, of Chicago. Though it seems unlikely that the Venetian artist could have seen the great navigator, who left Italy never to return, in 1479, the canvas is certainly that of a cosmographer, as indicated by the charts and books upon which his hand is resting.

The Metropolitan Museum of New York possesses still another canvas, bearing the inscription: *Haec est effigies Liguri miranda Colombi antipodum primus rate qui penetravit in orben. Sebastianus Venetus fecit.*

This last is a work of considerable genius, strikingly presented, the face feelingly drawn, and dating probably from the Romanesque period of Sebastiano del Piombo. In the other portraits, the Admiral stands bare-headed; here, he wears a hat with curled border, and an ornate mantle, deep-edged, hangs from his shoulders. The hands, however, and the pallid face, are those rather of some studious doctor of the Renaissance, than of the seaman. The person portrayed, moreover, seems to have been somewhere between forty and fifty years old; this, if it were Columbus, would place the portrait between the years 1490 and 1500. It was actually painted, however, about thirty years later.

Theodore de Bry, printer and engraved at Liège and Frankfort, in the sixteenth century published an engraving of Columbus, which he claimed to be a copy of a portrait painted by command of the King after the first voyage of the Admiral. It is, however, obviously a copy of the Piombo canvas.

Another portrait of Columbus has been attributed to Titian. This painting, in the possession of Mr. Sherman, at Rome, shows the figure in half-length, clad in a tunic of dark color, with a narrow white collar. This canvas was reproduced in 1506 by Caprioli, for his *Rittrati di cento capitani illustri*, and appears in the *Gazette des Beaux-Arts, 1922,* with *Les Portraits de Christophe Colomb,* by Gustave Soulier.

It shows a man of typical Venetian visage, with sallow skin, dark hair, and shrewd eye. It is probably by Titian, but almost certainly not of Columbus.

One must conclude, then, that in all probability no actual portrait of the Admiral exists today. All bear the characteristics of other races, according to the nationality of the artist—Venetian, Florentine or Liegeois. If we would construct in our own minds some image of the great discoverer we would do better to abandon these supposed likenesses and turn to those known to represent the face and characteristics of his Genoese contemporaries.

In those days, the hall of the Banca di San Giorgio contained the busts of the great leaders of the Republic. In 1508 Pace Gazini chiselled a likeness of Francesco Lomellino for this gallery, and from it we can picture something of the sort of man that was Columbus. The nose is high-arched, the expression strong and energetic, the impression given is one of intense purpose, reticent manner, inflexible will. And this, more than the romantic pictures the others painted, reveals the true character of the explorer-captain. He spoke the language and learned the ways of the country of his adoption, but his soul remained in Liguria to the last.

BIBLIOGRAPHY

The books printed about Columbus are more numerous, almost, than the waves of the seas he sailed over. No complete bibliography has ever been compiled. Henry Harisse gives the titles of those of ancient date in his *Bibliotheca americana vetustissima. A description of books relating to America published between the years 1492 and 1551*; New York 1886. Works in Spanish are listed in the *Bibliographia Colombina*, published at Madrid, 1892, by the *Real Academia de la Historia*.

A bibliography of Italian authors was prepared by Fumagalli, under the title: *Bibligrafia degli scritti italiani sopra Christopho Colombo*, and this was included in the collection made by the Italian Government in 1892, called the *Raccolta di documenti e studii, publicati della R. Commissione Colombiana*. This is the most complete bibliography of the subject, as well as of the Admiral's own writings, appearing up to that date.

At the end of the nineteenth century, two important studies were published: the *Christophe Colomb*, by Henry Harisse; Paris, 1884, and the *Etudes critiques sur la vie de Colomb avant ses Découvertes*, by Henry Vignaud; Paris, 1905. Both are works of great erudition and penetration. Vignaud also published, in 1911, an *Histoire critique de la grande entreprise de Christophe*

284

Colomb, a careful résumé of all the works appearing until that date on the navigator. Vignaud however, though a great student, was often led astray by his ideas. His matter is valuable, but his conclusions are sometimes to be avoided.

So far, no bibliography of the Dutch or the English authors has been compiled. Sir Clements Markham published a *Life of Christopher Columbus;* London, 1892. In America, the eminent historian John Boyd Thacher published his authoritative *Christopher Columbus;* New York, 1903-1904. In German, beside the earlier works of Humboldt, the best work on the subject is that by Sophus Ruge: *Columbus;* Berlin, 1903.

In France, in his *La Carte de Christophe Colomb;* Paris, 1924, Charles de la Roncière, the eminent historian of the French marine, published a chart found in the Bibliothèque Nationale and attributed to Columbus' hand.

The Genoese scholar, the Marchese Guiseppe Pesagno, revealed in his *Questioni Colombiane,* published in 1926, a number of hitherto unknown details concerning the early travels of Columbus, as uncovered by research in the archives of Genoa.

Among those at variance with the theory of his Genoese origin must be cited Don Ricardo Beltran y Rozpida, whose *Cristobal Colon;* Madrid, 1921, maintains that the discoverer, though born in Genoa, was of Spanish parentage; and the Doctor E. Martinez Lopez, author of the *Christobal Colon era español;* Honduras, 1925, who was convinced that Columbus, both in birth and parentage, was entirely Spanish. In the light of recent discoveries, as well as the numerous instances in which contemporaries spoke of the Admiral as a Genoese, these assertions will hardly hold water. The welcome with which Spain received his projects is in itself sufficient for her glory.

THIS BOOK WAS DESIGNED BY ROBERT S. JOSEPHY
AND PRINTED UNDER HIS SUPERVISION BY THE
J. J. LITTLE & IVES COMPANY, NEW YORK

AM

· AMERICVS · VESPVCIVS · FLORENTINVS ·

FLORA

Massa

Fiorenza

P. Vener

Spetia

P. Fin